CONOR McPHERSON

Conor McPherson was born in Dublin in 1971 and attended University College Dublin, where he began to write and direct. Original stage plays include *Rum & Vodka*, *The Good Thief*, *This Lime Tree Bower*, *St Nicholas*, *The Weir* (Olivier, Evening Standard and Critics' Circle Awards), *Dublin Carol*, *Port Authority*, *Shining City* (Tony Award-nominated), *The Seafarer* (Tony, Olivier and Evening Standard Award nominations), *The Veil* and *The Night Alive* (New York Drama Critics' Circle Award for Best Play). Theatre adaptations include Daphne du Maurier's *The Birds* (Gate Theatre, Dublin and Guthrie Theater, Minneapolis), August Strindberg's *The Dance of Death* (Donmar at Trafalgar Studios), Franz Xaver Kroetz's *The Nest* (Young Vic, London), and Paweł Pawlikowski's *Cold War* (Almeida Theatre, 2023). His 2020 adaptation of Chekhov's *Uncle Vanya* won the South Bank Show Sky Arts Theatre Award and was broadcast by BBC TV and PBS in the United States.

His collaboration with Bob Dylan, *Girl from the North Country*, opened at The Old Vic, London, before transferring to the West End (winning two Olivier Awards) and Broadway, where it was nominated for seven Tony Awards, including Best Musical, Best Director, Best Book of a Musical, and won the Tony for Best Orchestrations.

Awards for his screenwriting include four Best Screenplay Awards from the Irish Film and Television Academy; Spanish Screenwriters' Circle Best Screenplay Award; the CICAE award for Best Film from the Berlin Film Festival; the Jury Prize from the San Sebastián Film Festival; and the Méliès d'argent award for Best European Film.

Other Titles in this Series

Mike Bartlett
THE 47TH
ALBION
BULL
GAME
AN INTERVENTION
KING CHARLES III
MIKE BARTLETT PLAYS: TWO
MRS DELGADO
SCANDALTOWN
SNOWFLAKE
UNICORN
VASSA *after* Gorky
WILD

Chris Bush
THE ASSASSINATION OF KATIE HOPKINS
    with Matt Winkworth
THE CHANGING ROOM
CHRIS BUSH PLAYS: ONE
A DOLL'S HOUSE *after* Ibsen
FAUSTUS: THAT DAMNED WOMAN
HUNGRY
JANE EYRE *after* Brontë
THE LAST NOËL
OTHERLAND
ROBIN HOOD AND THE
    CHRISTMAS HEIST
    with Matt Winkworth
ROCK / PAPER / SCISSORS
STANDING AT THE SKY'S EDGE
    with Richard Hawley
STEEL

Jez Butterworth
THE FERRYMAN
THE HILLS OF CALIFORNIA
JERUSALEM
JEZ BUTTERWORTH PLAYS: ONE
JEZ BUTTERWORTH PLAYS: TWO
MOJO
THE NIGHT HERON
PARLOUR SONG
THE RIVER
THE WINTERLING

Caryl Churchill
BLUE HEART
CHURCHILL PLAYS: THREE
CHURCHILL PLAYS: FOUR
CHURCHILL PLAYS: FIVE
CHURCHILL: SHORTS
CLOUD NINE
DING DONG THE WICKED
A DREAM PLAY *after* Strindberg
DRUNK ENOUGH TO SAY I LOVE YOU?
ESCAPED ALONE
FAR AWAY
GLASS. KILL. BLUEBEARD'S FRIENDS.
IMP.
HERE WE GO
HOTEL
ICECREAM
LIGHT SHINING IN
    BUCKINGHAMSHIRE
LOVE AND INFORMATION
MAD FOREST
A NUMBER
PIGS AND DOGS
SEVEN JEWISH CHILDREN
THE SKRIKER
THIS IS A CHAIR
THYESTES *after* Seneca
TRAPS
WHAT IF IF ONLY

Natasha Gordon
NINE NIGHT

Lucy Kirkwood
BEAUTY AND THE BEAST
    with Katie Mitchell
BLOODY WIMMIN
THE CHILDREN
CHIMERICA
HEDDA *after* Ibsen
THE HUMAN BODY
IT FELT EMPTY WHEN THE HEART
    WENT AT FIRST BUT IT IS
    ALRIGHT NOW
LUCY KIRKWOOD PLAYS: ONE
MOSQUITOES
NSFW
RAPTURE
TINDERBOX
THE WELKIN

Conor McPherson
COLD WAR *after* Paweł Pawlikowski
DUBLIN CAROL
GIRL FROM THE NORTH COUNTRY
    with Bob Dylan
McPHERSON PLAYS: ONE
McPHERSON PLAYS: TWO
McPHERSON PLAYS: THREE
THE NEST *after* Franz Xaver Kroetz
THE NIGHT ALIVE
PORT AUTHORITY
THE SEAFARER
SHINING CITY
UNCLE VANYA *after* Chekhov
THE VEIL
THE WEIR

Jack Thorne
2ND MAY 1997
AFTER LIFE *after* Hirokazu Kore-eda
BUNNY
BURYING YOUR BROTHER IN
    THE PAVEMENT
A CHRISTMAS CAROL *after* Dickens
THE END OF HISTORY…
HOPE
JACK THORNE PLAYS: ONE
JACK THORNE PLAYS: TWO
JUNKYARD
LET THE RIGHT ONE IN
    after John Ajvide Lindqvist
THE MOTIVE AND THE CUE
MYDIDAE
THE SOLID LIFE OF SUGAR WATER
STACY & FANNY AND FAGGOT
WHEN YOU CURE ME
WHEN WINSTON WENT TO WAR WITH
    THE WIRELESS
WOYZECK *after* Büchner

debbie tucker green
BORN BAD
DEBBIE TUCKER GREEN PLAYS: ONE
DIRTY BUTTERFLY
EAR FOR EYE
HANG
NUT
A PROFOUNDLY AFFECTIONATE,
    PASSIONATE DEVOTION TO
    SOMEONE (– *NOUN*)
RANDOM
STONING MARY
TRADE & GENERATIONS
TRUTH AND RECONCILIATION

Conor McPherson

THE BRIGHTENING AIR

NICK HERN BOOKS

London

www.nickhernbooks.co.uk

A Nick Hern Book

The Brightening Air first published in Great Britain in 2025 as a paperback original by Nick Hern Books Limited, The Glasshouse, 49a Goldhawk Road, London W12 8QP

The Brightening Air copyright © 2025 Conor McPherson

Conor McPherson has asserted his right to be identified as the author of this work

Front cover: Joseph Mallord William Turner, *Lake Albano*, National Galleries of Scotland

Designed and typeset by Nick Hern Books, London
Printed in Great Britain by Mimeo Ltd, Huntingdon, Cambridgeshire PE29 6XX

A CIP catalogue record for this book is available from the British Library

ISBN 978 1 83904 419 9

CAUTION   All rights whatsoever in this play are strictly reserved. Requests to reproduce the text in whole or in part should be addressed to the publisher.

Amateur Performing Rights   Applications for performance, including readings and excerpts, by amateurs in the English language throughout the world should be addressed to the Performing Rights Manager, Nick Hern Books, The Glasshouse, 49a Goldhawk Road, London W12 8QP, *tel* +44 (0)20 8749 4953, *email* rights@nickhernbooks.co.uk, except as follows:

Australia: ORiGiN Theatrical, *email* enquiries@originmusic.com.au, *web* www.origintheatrical.com.au

New Zealand: Play Bureau, 20 Rua Street, Mangapapa, Gisborne, 4010, *tel* +64 21 258 3998, *email* info@playbureau.com

United States of America and Canada: Curtis Brown Ltd, see details below.

Professional Performing Rights   Application for performance by professionals in any medium and in any language throughout the world should be addressed to Curtis Brown Ltd, Cunard House, 15 Regent Street, St. James's, London SW1Y 4LR, *tel* +44 (0)20 7393 4400, *fax* +44 (0)20 7393 4401, *email* cb@curtisbrown.co.uk

No performance of any kind may be given unless a licence has been obtained. Applications should be made before rehearsals begin. Publication of this play does not necessarily indicate its availability for amateur performance.

www.nickhernbooks.co.uk/environmental-policy

Nick Hern Books' authorised representative in the EU is
Easy Access System Europe – Mustamäe tee 50, 10621 Tallinn, Estonia
email gpsr.requests@easproject.com

The Brightening Air was first performed at The Old Vic, London, on 10 April 2025, with the following cast:

ELIZABETH	Derbhle Crotty
BRENDAN	Eimhin Fitzgerald Doherty
STEPHEN	Brian Gleeson
FREYA	Aisling Kearns
FATHER PIERRE	Seán McGinley
LYDIA	Hannah Morrish
DERMOT	Chris O'Dowd
BILLIE	Rosie Sheehy

UNDERSTUDIES
BILLIE/FREYA	Ella Maria Carmen
BRENDAN/STEPHEN	Callum Cronin
DERMOT/FATHER PIERRE	Joseph McCarthy
ELIZABETH/LYDIA	Amy Vicary-Smith

Director	Conor McPherson
Set & Costume	Rae Smith
Lighting	Mark Henderson
Sound	Gregory Clarke
Movement & Intimacy	Lucy Hind
Casting	Serena Hill CDG
Voice	Charlie Hughes-D'Aeth
Dialect	Danièle Lydon
Fights	Kate Waters
Associate Director	Anastasia Osei-Kuffour
Associate Set	Niall McKeever
Costume Supervisor	Poppy Hall
Wigs, Hair & Make-Up Supervisor	Kim Kasim
Props Supervisor	Fahmida Bakht
Music Associate	Ben McQuigg
Company Stage Manager	Laura Draper
Deputy Stage Manager	Fran O'Donnell
Assistant Stage Manager (Book Cover)	Sophie Alice Cooper

It had become a glimmering girl
With apple blossom in her hair
Who called me by my name and ran
And faded through the brightening air.

William Butler Yeats

Characters

BILLIE, *late twenties*
STEPHEN, *her brother, early forties*
DERMOT, *brother to Billie and Stephen, forties*
LYDIA, *married to Dermot, forties*
FATHER PIERRE, *uncle to Billie, Stephen and Dermot, sixties*

ELIZABETH, *housekeeper to Father Pierre, fifties*
FREYA, *café waitress, twenties*
BRENDAN, *a farmer and barman, twenties*

Setting

A large house in the countryside in Ireland, 1981.

Note on Text

Words in [square brackets] are unspoken.

This text went to press before the end of rehearsals and so may differ slightly from the play as performed.

ACT ONE

A large room in an old house in the country. A generous bay window looking out at bare trees. A piano. The carpet is worn. The furniture is tired.

It's late afternoon. LYDIA *and* BILLIE *are carrying food and plates into a table set for drinks, snacks and sandwiches.*

LYDIA. Put these up the far end.

BILLIE. Can we talk?

LYDIA. Set the table and you can talk about whatever you want.

BILLIE. You start.

LYDIA. Okay. Stations.

BILLIE. Yeah – go.

LYDIA. Limerick Junction.

BILLIE. Yeah.

LYDIA. Talk to me.

BILLIE. There's no town there. Just a station. No one lives there. No one stays there. You just transfer.

LYDIA. You come and go.

BILLIE. Yeah, go anywhere. Like to a real place.

LYDIA. Escape anywhere.

BILLIE. Yeah, no one would know which way you went.

LYDIA (*frowns*). There's no town there?

BILLIE. There's nothing there. It's the middle of Tipperary. It's like a magic door. Get yourself a ticket to Limerick Junction, change platforms, and poof – you're gone!

LYDIA. Boom.

BILLIE. Shoot across to Rosslare Harbour. Ferry to Le Havre. SNCF to Paris, Orient Express to Istanbul – if you don't mind changing at Bucharest.

LYDIA. No, I don't mind.

BILLIE. Okay – well, once a week I think it is – there's a service to Tehran. Get yourself down there – through Iran, across Pakistan, bang, down into New Delhi, on to Varanasi. You know what's there, of course?

LYDIA. No.

BILLIE. In Varanasi? The Manikarnika Ghat. Where the steps lead down to the River Ganges. They cremate the bodies of the dead there twenty-four hours a day, seven days a week. You wanna be cremated there, Lydia, you know why?

LYDIA. Why?

BILLIE. 'Cause if you're burned there and your bones are thrown in the River Ganges – you won't be reincarnated any more, you're free. Your soul is washed clean, and you finally return to nothingness. With none of this life stuck on you any more.

LYDIA. I must do that then.

BILLIE. Yup – just get a ticket for Limerick Junction and off you go. Where will I put the cake?

LYDIA. In the middle.

BILLIE. Pride of place. Should we test it? Do a taste test.

LYDIA. You will not! You'll have your lunch with everyone else.

BILLIE. Lunch? It's five o'clock.

LYDIA. Late lunch.

BILLIE. Dinner.

LYDIA. Early dinner.

BILLIE. Linner. Lunner.

LYDIA. Dinch.

BILLIE. Dunch.

ACT ONE   11

A tired-looking man in his forties comes through.

STEPHEN. What are you doing?

LYDIA. Setting the table.

STEPHEN. For what?

LYDIA. What do you mean, for what?

STEPHEN. For who?

LYDIA. For your uncle. For when everyone is here. What do you think?

STEPHEN. Billie, you left the gate open, your chickens are all over the shop.

BILLIE. What?!

STEPHEN. I told you a million times.

BILLIE (*going*). And you can tell me a billion times and I still won't do it. So, understand that.

STEPHEN. Stupidity's beyond understanding.

BILLIE. That's why you're so thick.

She's gone.

LYDIA. This was my idea. Don't take it out on her.

STEPHEN. Take what out?

LYDIA *just looks at him. He bites a sandwich. She changes the subject.*

LYDIA. Billie seems good.

STEPHEN. Her fingers are all bent.

LYDIA. Yes, I saw.

STEPHEN. She won't go to physiotherapy unless I let her go on the train.

LYDIA. You won't let her?

STEPHEN. She can't manage on her own. She'll get to Sligo, walk out of the station, get hit by another car.

LYDIA. I could go with her.

STEPHEN. She won't let anyone go with her. It's impossible.

LYDIA. I know.

STEPHEN. Do you?

LYDIA drops it. Watches him for a moment.

LYDIA. So look. Dermot's coming.

STEPHEN. What here?

LYDIA. Mm. See your uncle. See everyone.

STEPHEN. See everyone?

LYDIA. He loves you, Stephen. He loves Billie.

STEPHEN. Yeah. He loves Billie.

He looks out the window.

LYDIA. See how you've been. How have you been?

STEPHEN. I'm great. How have you been?

LYDIA. Good. Yeah. I must get some of your eggs.

STEPHEN. Eggs is Billie.

LYDIA. Place looks well.

STEPHEN. It's cold.

LYDIA. It's a bit cold.

STEPHEN. Wind gets in everywhere. Rain gets in.

LYDIA. Has Dermot said anything?

STEPHEN. Said what?

LYDIA. Dermot. And your uncle.

STEPHEN. What?

LYDIA. I'll let them tell you.

STEPHEN. Tell me what?

LYDIA. Nothing.

STEPHEN. They want to sell. Get me and Billie out to sell it.

LYDIA. No, I don't think so.

STEPHEN. Then what?

LYDIA (*has had enough*). I said I'll let them tell you!

STEPHEN. That's why everyone's coming. I wouldn't mind but I've tried to get him to sell it to me. Buy them out. They won't sell it.

LYDIA. What if he wants to sell it to someone else?

STEPHEN. Is that what they said?

LYDIA. No, I don't – No.

STEPHEN. Then what?

LYDIA. Something. I don't know. But not selling it.

STEPHEN. Yeah, something. Then fuck him. I'll find us somewhere.

LYDIA. You'll always keep Billie with you, of course.

STEPHEN. What choice do I have?

LYDIA. She could stay with us.

STEPHEN (*sarcastic*). Yeah, right. If they try to fucking sell this… they'll… Let them try. (*Changes the subject.*) So how have you been? Did I ask you that? What's going on?

LYDIA. Nothing. The usual.

STEPHEN. All the usual.

LYDIA. Mm.

STEPHEN. Life and the whole lot.

LYDIA. Dermot's wandering again, you probably know that. So what's new?

STEPHEN. Yeah?

LYDIA. My own fault, of course. For giving him so many chances.

STEPHEN (*shakes his head*). He was always like that.

LYDIA (*a little laugh*). You might have told me!

STEPHEN. There *was* no telling you.

LYDIA. He's gone in the head. Girl over in Annaduff. We never see him. I've asked him what are we going to do. Says he doesn't know.

STEPHEN. Kick him out.

LYDIA. We have two children! I can't kick him out.

STEPHEN. Kids'll still have him. He won't be dead.

LYDIA. He's as upset as I am.

STEPHEN. Yeah… Give me a break.

LYDIA. Maybe you could…

STEPHEN. Maybe what? He doesn't talk to me.

LYDIA (*smiles*). Do you remember when we were younger? You told me about the water from the well up there in the fox's covert?

STEPHEN *gives a little laugh*.

Do you remember?

STEPHEN *nods*.

You said it could make someone fall in love with you.

STEPHEN *nods*.

Can you get me some?

STEPHEN. Are you serious?

LYDIA. You don't believe in it?

STEPHEN. Believe in it? Can't say I ever think about it.

LYDIA. Never think about love?

STEPHEN. No.

LYDIA. So this is it. You're just gonna take care of your sister. Live on your own. Dinner for one. Dinner for two.

STEPHEN. Looks like it.

LYDIA (*comes and picks some dirt off his jacket*). It's mad, isn't it?

STEPHEN. What is?

LYDIA. I married the brother who can't get enough. And here's you, you don't want any.

STEPHEN. Maybe there's nothing left for anyone to have.

She looks at him. Walks away.

LYDIA. Will you get me some?

STEPHEN. Some what? Some of the water?

LYDIA. From the well.

STEPHEN. I'll get it for five hundred pounds.

LYDIA. Five hundred pounds?!

STEPHEN. You can get it yourself if you want.

LYDIA. Okay, I will. Where is it exactly?

STEPHEN. You wouldn't even know it even if you were looking at it. It's just a trickle in the muck and the stones, in among the briars and the hawthorn. Little brass tap. I'd have to mow a way in. It's two days' work.

LYDIA. There's a tap?

STEPHEN. Tiny little brass tap someone put there years ago. Centuries ago. I don't know.

LYDIA. Five hundred pounds. Are you just punishing me?

STEPHEN. Why would I punish you? We were children.

LYDIA. Yeah well. Old pain lingers. Turns into arthritis.

STEPHEN. Not if you never feel anything any more. Did you put mustard on this?

LYDIA. You all love mustard.

STEPHEN. It's good.

LYDIA. Does it work?

STEPHEN. Yeah, it's nice.

LYDIA. I mean the water.

STEPHEN. They say you put it in his milk. Never in alcohol. Drink some when he drinks it. Say a Hail Mary.

LYDIA. A Hail Mary?!

STEPHEN. Or something – whatever. Say something. I don't know. I always heard it was a Hail Mary. And then you have to be the first person he sees when he wakes up. And that's it.

LYDIA. You've never tried it?

STEPHEN. Five hundred pound. Look I can't say fairer than that. It's a day and a night digging in there, I'll have the face and hands cut off me.

LYDIA (*tone of 'So what?'*). Well.

STEPHEN. To bewitch your own husband.

LYDIA. I'd only be doing it for the children.

STEPHEN (*dismissive*). Yeah. You're mad in your fucking head.

LYDIA. Will you get it for me?

ELIZABETH. Here you all are!

They turn to see a handsome woman of about fifty in the doorway.

LYDIA. Elizabeth! Look at you.

ELIZABETH. And look at you all.

LYDIA. We never heard you coming.

ELIZABETH. We parked at the bottom of the driveway. Father Pierre wanted to walk up.

LYDIA. Can he find his way?

ELIZABETH. He's feeling his way along with his stick.

LYDIA. What can he see?

ELIZABETH. Vague light and shadow.

STEPHEN. His nose will lead him to the damp.

ELIZABETH. How are you, Stephen?

STEPHEN. I'm fantastic.

ELIZABETH. And Billie?

STEPHEN. She's rocking.

ELIZABETH (*putting down a bag or two*). He wants to say mass while he's here. I'm telling you now before he gets here.

STEPHEN. No problem.

ELIZABETH. He was worried that...

STEPHEN. No problem. He can say mass every day if he likes.

ELIZABETH. He rarely gets the opportunity any more. I mean he says mass with me there.

LYDIA. Just the two of you?

ELIZABETH. Yes, every morning after breakfast in the living room. You know the parish don't pay my wages any more?

LYDIA. That's terrible.

ELIZABETH. But I couldn't leave him on his own. I was offered another job but...

LYDIA. No.

ELIZABETH. He can't do anything for himself.

STEPHEN. You're like an old married couple.

ELIZABETH. I suppose we are!

LYDIA. They should allow marriage for priests.

ELIZABETH. I don't want to marry him, Lydia!

LYDIA. No, I mean...

ELIZABETH. I'm his housekeeper.

LYDIA. No, that's... I just mean – in general.

FATHER PIERRE. Look who I found!

BILLIE *leads* FATHER PIERRE *in*.

BILLIE. He walked in cowshite twice!

ELIZABETH (*coming to* FATHER PIERRE, *pulling at his dirty trousers*). What? Ah look at you!

FATHER PIERRE (*embarrassed, fiercely*). Get off me! It's fine. (*Suddenly cordial.*) Look who's here! Who's here?

LYDIA. Me, Father – Lydia, Dermot's wife.

FATHER PIERRE. Dermot's wife!

LYDIA. Lydia.

FATHER PIERRE. Yes, yes. And Dermot!

LYDIA. No, it's Stephen.

STEPHEN. The younger one.

ELIZABETH. The handsome one.

FATHER PIERRE. Yes, I know, I know! Stephen. And Billie is here. Look at the size of her! Who else – did you never get married, Stephen?

STEPHEN. Not yet no.

FATHER PIERRE. And you're running the place?

STEPHEN. Me and Billie.

BILLIE. I do the chickens. How did you get here?

ELIZABETH. In the car.

BILLIE. From Dublin?

ELIZABETH. From Dundalk.

BILLIE. Dundalk? You coulda shot down the Belfast line. Transfer at Connolly. Like it's literally the same fricking platform!

LYDIA. Are you hungry? You must be!

FATHER PIERRE. Is there food? I can smell it. Yes!

LYDIA. Let me get you a plate. Sit down. Stephen, why are there no chairs?

STEPHEN. We never sit in here.

BILLIE. We sit in the kitchen. We live in the kitchen.

LYDIA. Billie, get some chairs. Stephen!

STEPHEN *and* BILLIE *go to get some chairs.*

FATHER PIERRE. By Christ, that's some smell of spiders. Don't they heat the place?

ELIZABETH. It's just the two of them.

FATHER PIERRE. Like two children minding a house. This was where we used to spend all our time. When I was a boy. With their father, my brother Teddy, in here, studying – wrestling on the floor. There was our old great-uncle Séamus, asleep in a bed in the corner – he never woke up, so we'd come in here to hide from our dad. But he'd always find us. He'd come in and wrestle us. In here. He tried a mad crazy new kick on me one time. Had to have my two front teeth taken out. My gums were purple. He tried it on my brother – on Teddy – Teddy went deaf in one ear.

ELIZABETH. God, that's a terrible story.

FATHER PIERRE. That's life. That's… The roars were so violent, our great-uncle Séamus even woke up – once or twice – always wanging on about the covert out there. How an old hunchback, an old ancestor of ours, was cured by the fairies – but didn't he go back – to ask for more favours – so they gave him two humps! And how is Dermot, Lydia?

LYDIA. Yes, he's very well.

FATHER PIERRE. Devoted to your children.

LYDIA. Yes.

FATHER PIERRE. Devoted to you.

LYDIA. Yes.

FATHER PIERRE. Thank God.

LYDIA. Elizabeth was saying you still say mass every day.

FATHER PIERRE. Yes. It's a form of meditation now really. No congregation when they retire you off. I'm never compelled to give a sermon now. But I might – if we have a little mass here.

LYDIA. Yes, well, Dermot is coming – I can't think what's keeping him – he'd love to see you.

FATHER PIERRE. Lovely. Yes, I'd like to catch up with him.

ELIZABETH. Have a catch-up...

FATHER PIERRE. About everything... What the state of play is.

LYDIA. Stephen and Billie live here.

FATHER PIERRE. I know.

ELIZABETH. But to get his advice.

FATHER PIERRE. He's knitted in so well to the business community and the market and...

LYDIA. Oh yes.

FATHER PIERRE. What'd be best for the place and... I mean, with this pair in charge here, I mean...

ELIZABETH. There's a bird's nest out there in the hallway.

STEPHEN. No.

FATHER PIERRE. What?!

ELIZABETH. Yes – up in the cornicing.

FATHER PIERRE. I mean, this is what I'm...

    STEPHEN *and* BILLIE *carry in some chairs.*

LYDIA (*eating*). Do you like these?

ELIZABETH. What is it? Mushroom?

LYDIA. And cream.

FATHER PIERRE. Oh, cream!

ELIZABETH. Billie, what are you wearing, my love?

BILLIE. Work clothes.

ELIZABETH. Have you good clothes?

BILLIE. These are all my clothes. I always look like this.

ELIZABETH. Stephen, has she nothing else to wear for the day that's in it?

STEPHEN. I honestly couldn't tell you.

ELIZABETH. Wouldn't you buy her something nice?

STEPHEN. With what?

ELIZABETH (*sarcastic*). Oh yeah.

STEPHEN. Have you any idea what this place costs us just to turn on the lights?

ELIZABETH. Didn't you get that nice cheque Father Pierre sent you?

STEPHEN. When?

FATHER PIERRE. Now, Elizabeth.

ELIZABETH. I do his accounts. We sent you two thousand pounds.

STEPHEN. Who's we?

ELIZABETH. From Father Pierre's account, I sent the cheque. He signed it, I sent it to the account here in town so we're the 'we'.

BILLIE (*laughs*). We're the wee.

LYDIA. I'm sure Stephen used it to mind everything.

STEPHEN. Bank woulda shoved it straight into the overdraft. You shoulda sent cash.

FATHER PIERRE. I'm sure we can... Elizabeth. She's tired. We're all tired.

They fall silent as a young woman, FREYA, comes in, carrying some groceries.

FREYA. Hello.

DERMOT. What have I missed?

They turn to see DERMOT coming in.

FATHER PIERRE. Dermot!

DERMOT. Father. (*To* LYDIA.) Are the kids here?

LYDIA. No.

DERMOT. But you're here. And I'm... And everybody's... Freya, come in, come in, that's right. This is Freya, she... works in our... for us. I thought we could use the help.

FREYA *steps in further, uncertainly.*

FREYA. Does anyone want tea? Will I pour it?

DERMOT *looks at the table. There is no tea.*

DERMOT. Lydia, will you make some tea so Freya can...

LYDIA. We'll have tea after. There's drinks here. There's orange, water, we'll have tea after with some cake.

FREYA. Let me get you a plate of sandwiches, Father.

FREYA *sets about piling sandwiches on a plate.*

BILLIE. Did youse come on the...

DERMOT. No.

BILLIE. The eleven-forty.

DERMOT. No, like, from where? We came in the car.

BILLIE. Can we...

DERMOT. No, sorry, Father – how are you?

FATHER PIERRE. Dermot, my old...

His face suddenly crumples and he silently weeps.

DERMOT. What? Now now, there you go.

ELIZABETH. He's tired.

FATHER PIERRE. Dermot, you have no idea...

DERMOT. It's good to see you. Billie – get a napkin.

FATHER PIERRE. Sorry, no, I'm fine.

DERMOT. Have a sandwich.

FATHER PIERRE. Yes, I'll...

DERMOT. Get the blood sugar up. And, Freya, where's the – We have an apple tart. Lydia, plate that up. Freya, give it to Lydia. Lydia, have you any paracetamol? My head is killing me.

LYDIA *thumps a chair down and goes out.*

ELIZABETH. Isn't it very humid?

FREYA. We saw lightning.

DERMOT. And thunder.

BILLIE. You don't see thunder.

FREYA. Can I get anyone a sandwich?

FATHER PIERRE. Who is this?

FREYA. I'm Freya.

DERMOT. She works in my café. One of the cafés.

ELIZABETH. You live in the...

FREYA. I live in Annaduff.

ELIZABETH. Oh very nice.

DERMOT. We have so many young people coming and going. Faceless, you know...

FATHER PIERRE. No character.

DERMOT. Now. But when I saw Freya in action, I said to myself, 'Now, *that's* interesting.'

They sit in the motley selection of chairs that BILLIE *and* STEPHEN *have foraged, in an irregular clump round the room, like people sitting in a waiting room at a train station rather than a cosy abode.*

FATHER PIERRE. When you see it.

DERMOT. When you see it. That's half the battle. A nose for people. I keep her with me now. She's indispensable.

LYDIA (*coming back with some tablets for* DERMOT). Have you finished school, Freya?

FREYA. I have a diploma in hotel management.

DERMOT. She's management material.

LYDIA. Seems a bit of waste to drag her out here to serve sandwiches.

DERMOT. That's management too, Lydia. You wouldn't understand. (*To* FATHER PIERRE.) This is what I'm up against. So, Stephen, place is like a fuckin' tip as usual.

LYDIA. Dermot!

DERMOT. This is how we communicate! Isn't it? Come here!

DERMOT grabs STEPHEN, tries to get him in a headlock. STEPHEN forcefully resists. DERMOT bangs against the table.

LYDIA (*shouts*). Dermot, what are you doing?

DERMOT (*shaking his fingers, clenching and unclenching his fist*). Alright, Stephen, no need to lose the noodle! We're always messing like this.

FATHER PIERRE. Horseplay. There's nothing like it!

DERMOT. The gate's hanging off the hinges.

STEPHEN. Yeah. The lad who helps me with the milking hit it in the dark the other morning.

DERMOT. Whatcha need help with the milking for?

STEPHEN. I just do.

DERMOT. Freya, can you give people… make sure everyone has a drink. There's Paddy Powers in that bag.

FATHER PIERRE. Oh!

LYDIA. Dermot, it's only, what is it? Is it five o'clock?

DERMOT. Five o'clock is fine! It's fine! Pierre can turn it into the consecrated blood of Christ.

FATHER PIERRE. Wine – not whiskey.

DERMOT. It'll be strong blood. The blood of Christ.

ELIZABETH. I assume that would be some kind of sacrilege.

DERMOT. Yes – sacrilege to mess about with good whiskey – I agree.

LYDIA (*to* FREYA). Has he had some already?

FREYA nods.

DERMOT. Stephen won't say no.

BILLIE. And I won't say no.

DERMOT. Put lemonade in it.

STEPHEN. Billie, no.

BILLIE. Ah, fuck off, Stephen, you're only an old fucking granny.

ELIZABETH. Billie.

BILLIE. What? You're a guest here. This is how we speak. We communicate with each other here.

ELIZABETH. Your uncle is a man of the cloth.

BILLIE (*shrugs*). I don't believe in any of that bollocks.

LYDIA. Billie!

BILLIE. Here, Freya, this glass is fine. On top of my lemonade.

FREYA *looks to* DERMOT. DERMOT *nods*. LYDIA *looks to* STEPHEN. STEPHEN *shrugs*.

DERMOT. Father Pierre won't say no.

FATHER PIERRE. I will not.

DERMOT *sings softly, almost under his breath*. FATHER PIERRE *joining with him*.

DERMOT/FATHER PIERRE.
Do you love an apple?
Do you love a pear?
Do you love a laddie with bonny brown hair?
Still I love him. I can't deny him.
I'll be with him wherever he goes...

DERMOT (*to* FREYA, *who continues working*). Freya, sit down, will ya? You're like a crockery wasp.

FREYA *sits. They are all quiet*.

Now. Can you feel that?

BILLIE. Feel what?

DERMOT. That silence. This silence has been brought to you courtesy of Dermot McFaddin.

FATHER PIERRE. That smell, here. It's like nowhere else. This was my home, Billie, just as it's yours now. We were children out there in that greenery. In here. Me and your poor late father. My brother.

BILLIE. Well of course you were. You weren't born as adults.

FATHER PIERRE. No! But that smell. I mean, it must be the…

ELIZABETH. Every soil in every place must have its unique chemical composition.

FATHER PIERRE. Yes.

ELIZABETH. And smell being such a component part of memory…

BILLIE. Yes, evolution means you can survive if you can just find your way home.

FATHER PIERRE. That's the trick.

ELIZABETH. And we have. Father Pierre has.

DERMOT. You planning to stay a few days or…

FATHER PIERRE. Yeah – a few days! We're playing it by ear. We'll see.

DERMOT. Yeah, good, great. I'm gonna bring you everywhere. Show you… I mean the influx of… in town, the boats in the marina. And the crypt in the church… (*To* ELIZABETH.) It's our family crypt. They've put on a new glass door. Our mother's grandparents are in there. Two bodies in there – the coffins are under glass. You can see them.

ELIZABETH. Oh. Yes, I've seen it. He had the crypt built when she died, didn't he?

FATHER PIERRE. Yes, to keep her safe. Till he could join her.

DERMOT. Makes sense.

BILLIE. Now they're both in there.

LYDIA. It's cold in there.

FATHER PIERRE. They don't mind!

BILLIE. I'd mind. I don't want to be there, in a church in the street where anyone and walk in and look at me.

ACT ONE   27

ELIZABETH. It wouldn't be you.

BILLIE. It would be me. This is me, this is all there is.

ELIZABETH (*disagreeing*). Well.

FREYA. Like he wanted him and his wife to be like...

BILLIE. Publicly displayed.

FREYA. No – safe. Away from the darkness in places...

DERMOT. Like places out here.

FREYA. Yeah, I don't know.

BILLIE. In the darkness of the hedges.

ELIZABETH. Hedges aren't dark.

BILLIE. They are at night.

FREYA. I think he wanted to feel protected in there in the middle of the people in the town.

BILLIE. Protected from what?

FREYA. The dark.

BILLIE. You wouldn't want to walk on a train track at night.

FATHER PIERRE. No!

DERMOT. Yeah, well, they sleep in there, now.

LYDIA. It's status as well of course.

DERMOT. Asleep in there forever.

BILLIE. What if they're not, though? What if everyone coming in and out to look at their coffins wakes them up – to realise their mistake.

ELIZABETH. What mistake?

BILLIE. Shoulda been buried in the ground so you don't wake up. Not left behind a glass door in the church with the door open and the traffic going by. Like – (*Makes a beeping noise.*) and they're lying there like... 'Well this was fucking'... [*a stupid idea.*]

ELIZABETH (*after a moment*). Well, this is lovely.

LYDIA. Well, look, why don't we get you sorted out. The rooms are aired.

DERMOT. Freya. Bags. (*To* ELIZABETH.) Where's your bags?

ELIZABETH. Oh. Billie?

BILLIE (*as though it's an obvious answer to a stupid question*). Outside!

DERMOT. Outside! What are they doing outside? It's raining, for fuck's sake, Billie.

BILLIE. It's not raining, Dermot. That's called drizzle. If you use your senses.

DERMOT. Get the bags! For fuck's sake. Sorry, Pierre.

FATHER PIERRE. They're good leather bags. Italian leather.

LYDIA. Come on, Billie.

DERMOT. No, Freya – help Lydia.

LYDIA *looks at* DERMOT.

That's what she's here for!

ELIZABETH. Right.

FATHER PIERRE. What are we doing?

ELIZABETH. Get you to your room, get you sorted out.

FATHER PIERRE. My room, my old room.

LYDIA. Which one was your room?

FATHER PIERRE. Front – down here.

BILLIE. That's my room, so...

LYDIA. Stephen has you up the back.

FATHER PIERRE. Up the back – over the kitchen passage?

LYDIA. It's quiet.

DERMOT. It's damp!

LYDIA. We put the electric heater on.

DERMOT. When?

STEPHEN. This morning.

DERMOT. This morning? You shoulda had it on since yesterday.

LYDIA. And Elizabeth across the way.

DERMOT. If you want your old room, Pierre.

ELIZABETH. There isn't any damp spores? If spores get down into his... then we're all...

STEPHEN. No.

DERMOT. Of course there will be. Billie, move your stuff and give Father Pierre his room, for fuck's sake.

BILLIE. I need my room. I'm not moving my stuff.

FATHER PIERRE. It's fine. I'm sure it's fine. It's only a few days.

LYDIA. Are you sure?

FATHER PIERRE. Our bags are in the rain!

FREYA. I'll get them.

FREYA goes.

DERMOT. Billie – get the bags.

BILLIE. Freya's getting them – that's what you brought her for.

ELIZABETH (*brightly*). Right!

LYDIA. Come on, we'll get you sorted.

FATHER PIERRE. And we'll be right as dodgers. See you shortly.

LYDIA. That's it, out this way, are you alright?

FATHER PIERRE. I nearly walked into the wall, ha ha!

BILLIE. Pity you're not a ghost.

FATHER PIERRE (*as* ELIZABETH *leads him out*). Yes. Well, I am. In a machine.

ELIZABETH (*absently as they go*). Ghost in the machine.

LYDIA *glances at* DERMOT *and goes with* ELIZABETH *and* FATHER PIERRE.

DERMOT. He'll get black lung up there over the kitchen passage.

STEPHEN. Yeah, well...

DERMOT (*getting a drink*). Here, do you want one?

STEPHEN *shakes his head.*

BILLIE. I will.

DERMOT. A small one – where's your lemonade? Put your lemonade in it.

BILLIE *gets lemonade.* DERMOT *pours drinks for himself and* BILLIE.

Stephen, the place is like a tip.

STEPHEN. What do you mean?

DERMOT. The gate's hanging off. Everything overgrown everywhere. Cowshite. The damp in here is like I can feel it on my face.

STEPHEN. What do you want me to do about it?

DERMOT. Mind the place, for fuck's sake! What are youse living here for? If you don't want to live here, move on out to fuck and we'll find someone who will look after it.

BILLIE. And live where? Go where?

DERMOT. I don't know. We'd get rent for this place – or sell it, get you a flat in town.

BILLIE. I don't want a flat in town! Where would the chickens live?

DERMOT. What chickens?

BILLIE. The chickens out there that give us the eggs.

DERMOT. I don't know.

STEPHEN. What do you care anyway? Only Father Pierre is here, you wouldn't have come up.

ACT ONE 31

DERMOT. Well, that's what I'm... I mean, have youse no dreams for yourselves? Live and die in the family home, your home of origin they call it, I mean it's...

BILLIE. What oranges?

DERMOT. Origin.

BILLIE. Oranging?

DERMOT. Home of origin.

BILLIE. Like, home?

DERMOT. Of origin.

STEPHEN. Where do you want us to live and die?

DERMOT. I don't care. You can stay here if you want – I'm not making you do anything.

STEPHEN. Well, you can't make us do anything, it's not your house, it's alls our house.

DERMOT. Yeah, I know.

STEPHEN. So...

DERMOT. I know!

STEPHEN. What are you fucking playing at anyway?

DERMOT. What.

BILLIE. What's the story with this young one?

DERMOT. That's Freya.

BILLIE. Yeah, I know.

STEPHEN. What are you...

DERMOT. I'm not anything.

STEPHEN. You fucking bring her in here under Lydia's nose – what you want to do that for?

DERMOT. She'll give us a hand! She does everything for me. You've no idea the difference she's made.

STEPHEN. Yeah, I have some idea.

DERMOT. What's it to you anyhow? I'll give you a kick up the arse, mind your own business.

STEPHEN. You hitting the bottle and the whole lot?

DERMOT. Yeah, well, this is what I'm talking about. It's alright for you pair. Hanging about up here, fuckarsing around, and sitting in the kitchen listening to the radio all day long. I'm out there with a business and a family and the whole lot. No wonder I'm the way I am when I look at the pair of you.

BILLIE. What's that supposed to mean?

DERMOT. I see what I've had to overcome that's… You know.

STEPHEN. You've had to overcome being one of us.

DERMOT. Yeah, yeah, maybe I have. Maybe there's some things I'd do differently, I see that now. I don't want to hurt Lydia. I don't want to hurt my kids. But unfortunately for everybody – guess what? Dermot's alive too! And I've been getting up at the crack of dark – running my business – making sure everyone is alright. Paying for my house, not living in the one I grew up in like you. And maybe I came to a few conclusions like, 'What the fuck am I doing with my life? 'Cause, I sure as fuck amn't enjoying it! And I know youse don't want me up here.'

STEPHEN. Oh yeah, blame us.

DERMOT. Yeah – the older brother has to do it all, mate! You don't slip through the net like you two. Dad was all over my arse. You don't give a fuck. Why should you? I wouldn't care either if I was you. Anyway then, one day, there's a new girl in the café in Annaduff. And I dunno. Just her way about her, you know, the lightness and the directness how she spoke to everyone, just so disarming and fucking… no sides to her. You know? And I said to myself 'Now *that's* interesting… That's…' You know? And here it is as well –

He looks round quickly.

She's not like these fucking… She's like a boy in a girl's body…

STEPHEN (*to himself*). For fuck's sake…

DERMOT. In a good way! I mean it in a good way! I mean in how she might choose to just throw her hair up – and just go round in a T-shirt like she couldn't give a fuck! You know what I mean? I mean *that's...*

He laughs.

BILLIE. How old is she?

DERMOT. Difference that make?

BILLIE. I don't know. None, I suppose.

DERMOT. She's in her twenties. She's not...

BILLIE. How old though?

DERMOT. She's twenty.

STEPHEN *laughs.*

Yeah, big joke. I had to take her to London. She was in the family way.

STEPHEN. You're having me on.

DERMOT. No, took her over. It wasn't even mine. I swear. Told Lydia I was going on business. We got there, she changed her mind. Couldn't get her to go into the clinic. Came back. She changed her mind again. Over we went again. You've no idea what she's been through. On the Tube going out to Wood Green, load of Chelsea supporters come down the platform singing –

Sings to the air of 'She'll Be Coming Round the Mountain'.

'Would you like a chicken supper, Bobby Sands?
Would you like a chicken supper, Bobby Sands?
Would you like a chicken supper?
You dirty Irish fucker
Would you like a chicken supper, Bobby Sands...'

If they'd known we were Irish! I kept my mouth shut, I had enough trouble. Other than that, I would have...

STEPHEN. You would've what?

DERMOT. Well, I would've said something.

BILLIE *laughs. A young man,* BRENDAN, *is standing in the doorway.* BILLIE *sees him.*

BRENDAN. Hello… Sorry. Hiya, Billie. Hello.

DERMOT. Who's this?

BRENDAN. Hiya, Dermot. Brendan Byrne.

DERMOT. Brendan Byrne! Wouldya look at you, you're a big fine galoot! How's your mother?

BRENDAN. Yeah good thanks.

DERMOT. And the farm and the bar and the whole lot.

BRENDAN. Yeah, my mam is taking care of the bar. I do the rest.

DERMOT. Minding the cows.

BRENDAN. Mm.

DERMOT. And you're minding them here too?

BRENDAN. I'm giving a hand.

DERMOT. I get it – sure, why wouldn't ya? It's all adding up now.

FREYA *comes in.*

FREYA. Sorry, Dermot, Father Pierre is after falling.

DERMOT. What? Where?

FREYA. In the toilet.

DERMOT. Into the toilet?

FREYA. No, in the…

DERMOT (*going*). For fuck's sake. Is he alright?

FREYA. No, he's fine, we just need a hand helping him up.

STEPHEN *follows* DERMOT *and* FREYA *out, pausing at the door.*

STEPHEN. Brendan, can I sort you out later?

BRENDAN. Yeah, no, that's…

STEPHEN. It's all a bit mad here. I know I owe you, how much do I owe you?

BRENDAN. Yeah, no, it's fine, we'll sort it out later.

STEPHEN. I'll... Yeah, no worries. Just let me see what's going on here and I'll...

STEPHEN *goes*. BRENDAN *stands there while* BILLIE *helps herself to another drink of whiskey, topping it up with lemonade.*

BILLIE. You want a sandwich?

BRENDAN *comes to the table and starts eating.*

BRENDAN. It's nice. What's...

BILLIE. What's what?

BRENDAN. What's going on?

BILLIE. Our uncle has come to visit us. He was a priest.

BRENDAN. Oh yeah. Is he not any more?

BILLIE. He's retired or something. But he can't stay in my room so... I think he fell or something.

BRENDAN. Yeah...

BILLIE. Cows in?

BRENDAN. Mm. (*Laughs.*) Jaysus, Billie.

BILLIE (*laughs*). What?

BRENDAN. Will you not say anything?

BILLIE. Like what?

BRENDAN. You're not talking to me.

BILLIE. Can we talk about...

BRENDAN. We can talk about anything you like.

BILLIE. Okay. You go.

BRENDAN. Go what? Talk about what? Maps? I don't know enough... What? You tell me.

BILLIE. No, you.

BRENDAN. You never came.

BILLIE. Came where?

BRENDAN. Where we said. In town. At The County Hotel.

BILLIE. We said we'd meet at The County, yeah?

BRENDAN. Yeah, in the bar.

BILLIE. In the lounge.

BRENDAN. In the lounge, yeah. They only have a lounge.

BILLIE. Yeah, I couldn't.

BRENDAN. Well, I was waiting for you.

BILLIE. How was it?

BRENDAN (*laughs*). Awkward? Lonely!

BILLIE. So I didn't miss much.

BRENDAN. I suppose. You could have told me, though, if you couldn't come.

BILLIE. How?

BRENDAN. Phone?

BILLIE. Yeah and your mother picks up the phone. I'm not gonna phone you.

BRENDAN. Well, you could've told me.

BILLIE. I wasn't able to!

BRENDAN. Well, do you wanna meet me?

BILLIE. For what?

BRENDAN. For, I don't know. Do you like me?

BILLIE. Like what?

BRENDAN. My...

BILLIE. Your soul? Your essence.

BRENDAN. Yeah, whatever.

BILLIE. Your sense of humour? Your looks?

BRENDAN. Probably not my looks but, I don't know. I like you, Billie, what can I say? If I'm wasting my time, that's... I mean...

BILLIE. I don't wanna break your heart.

BRENDAN. I feel like it might be too late.

BILLIE. Whose fault is that?

BRENDAN. I don't know. Ah, Billie... I'm a person too, you know.

BILLIE. Yeah, I know.

BRENDAN. You're just using me.

BILLIE. When?

BRENDAN. When we were in the covert. When we... you know...

BILLIE. We were just using each other. So what?

BRENDAN. You don't want to be seen with me.

BILLIE. Who wants to be seen by anybody?

BRENDAN. Yeah, well... I just feel like you crush my feelings in the dirt.

BILLIE. The melodrama. I wasn't able to come, alright? And I won't be able.

BRENDAN. What do you mean 'not able'?

BILLIE. I mean, I'm not able to.

BRENDAN. Just say you don't want to.

BILLIE. I do want to! But I'm not able to! Alright? Some people just aren't able to do the things you want them to do! Alright?

BRENDAN. What, like you want to, but someone is stopping you? Or...?

BILLIE. I'm not able to! I'm not able to! I'm just not able to! Alright?! And here. Listen, when two people are together – you know – doing it –

She bangs her fists together.

It's supposed to be like this – the two people pushing towards each other at the same time – but when *you're* doing it, it's…

She moves her fists sideways together.

…like moving in the same direction, like away from me when I'm pushing into you, you know what I mean? You move like a swing going in the wrong direction! So, like nothing happens – it doesn't feel like anything! Like, what are you doing that for?

BRENDAN. Sorry, I…

BILLIE. That'd drive you mad! Like, come on!

LYDIA *comes in and realises she's in the gale force of* BILLIE*'s temper.*

LYDIA. Oh sorry, I'll…

BRENDAN. No, sorry, I'm…

BRENDAN *starts to go.*

BILLIE. Here, look, I'll meet you at The County. Do you want to meet?

BRENDAN. Nah, I can't… I'll… (*To* LYDIA *as he goes out.*) Sorry. I'll just…

BRENDAN *goes.*

LYDIA. So!

BILLIE. Yeah. So.

LYDIA. Father Pierre is alright. He just twisted his…

BILLIE. I don't care, Lydia.

BILLIE *stands looking out the window.*

LYDIA. Go after him.

BILLIE. No. I'm gonna put the chickens in.

STEPHEN *comes in.*

STEPHEN. Billie, put the chickens in, will ya?

BILLIE. I just said I'm doing it!

STEPHEN. Okay.

BILLIE. You fucking idiot.

She goes.

LYDIA. Will you get it for me?

STEPHEN. Get what?

LYDIA. The water. From the covert.

STEPHEN. You really want him.

LYDIA *nods*.

Five hundred pounds.

LYDIA. Yeah. Thank you.

STEPHEN. You're welcome.

She goes, leaving STEPHEN *standing there, looking out.*

Lights.

ACT TWO

The lights rise to find STEPHEN *and* ELIZABETH *wrapped in a curtain on the floor. She sits looking at him. He wakes up.* STEPHEN*'s hands are covered in plasters.*

ELIZABETH. Hello.

STEPHEN. What time is it?

ELIZABETH. About ten.

STEPHEN (*looking about*). Fucking hell.

ELIZABETH. I dreamt I was on a ship. We were rolling about in the cabin.

STEPHEN. Who was?

ELIZABETH. You and me. You were there. Do you not remember?

STEPHEN. Yeah, no, I do.

He gets up and finds his shirt. She watches him.

ELIZABETH. You know how long it's been since I saw you?

STEPHEN. How long?

ELIZABETH. You weren't counting the days? Four years.

STEPHEN. God.

ELIZABETH. I should be up there getting him his breakfast. But I can actually hear him snoring, listen.

STEPHEN *listens. Shakes his head.*

I can feel it. I've lived with that sound for thirty years. That vibration. He's out for the count. Billie won't come in here, will she?

STEPHEN. She never gets up till about twelve.

ACT TWO   41

ELIZABETH. You've never met anyone?

STEPHEN. Maybe I have.

ELIZABETH. Where is she?

STEPHEN. Where indeed.

ELIZABETH. I don't think so, here gimme one of those.

She takes a cigarette from a pack on the floor.

You smell of alone-ness.

STEPHEN. What does it smell like?

ELIZABETH. Smells lonely, Stephen.

STEPHEN. Not like you then, with old Uncle Pierre.

ELIZABETH. Just 'cause I live with him doesn't mean we're... I mean he's a priest.

STEPHEN. So? He's still a man.

ELIZABETH. That's true. When you're housekeeper to a priest it's like skipping the fun part of a marriage and just getting straight to the celibacies.

STEPHEN. Yeah but most housekeepers surely don't live with their... housekeepees.

ELIZABETH. No.

STEPHEN. Everybody must assume youse are...

ELIZABETH. They can assume away and imagine the worst – he's more or less excommunicated anyway so...

STEPHEN. That bad?

ELIZABETH. Not 'cause of me. That's as innocent as you'd ever... I mean, can you imagine?! No, but sure he's been at war with the men upstairs forever.

STEPHEN. Yeah?

ELIZABETH. Your whole family, you're all difficult, sure.

STEPHEN. Mm.

ELIZABETH. If not impossible.

STEPHEN. What, has he his own... religion or...

ELIZABETH. Ah, he has his own interpretation of the Bible and the whole lot. They had to stop him going round giving the last rites and everything. No one wanted him coming near them at the end. Too weird.

STEPHEN. Mm.

ELIZABETH. And that suits me and you're a bit like me too – I know you are.

STEPHEN. Mm?

ELIZABETH. You living with your sister. Me with a priest.

STEPHEN. Life's lost causes.

She laughs, gets up, looking for a drink.

ELIZABETH. Your brother is more functional than you, though. She's a nice woman, Lydia.

STEPHEN. Mm. Yeah right. Functionality is a sliding scale too, you know.

ELIZABETH. That girl he brought here yesterday, I mean, he's not...

STEPHEN. He's a dickhead.

ELIZABETH. And Lydia is so beautiful.

STEPHEN. He was always... He's the most like our dad out of the three of us. Our dad was like him. Kind of... mentally... fucking...

ELIZABETH. Not like you.

STEPHEN. No. Well, I hope not.

ELIZABETH. What do you do all day?

STEPHEN. When?

ELIZABETH. When you're here all day – with Billie.

STEPHEN. I mind Billie.

ELIZABETH. And what else.

STEPHEN. Like what?

ELIZABETH. Like what! Do you read? Go to the pictures? Drink? What do you do?

STEPHEN. Tidy up. Tell Billie to wash herself. Give her some lunch. Tell her to get dressed. Make sure Brendan's done the cows. Get the shopping. Get the dinner. We sit in the kitchen. Radio always on. She listens to the charts. I walk out there.

ELIZABETH. Where do you go? Tell me.

STEPHEN. Up out to the fox's covert, look out at the river. That just about takes care of the day, Elizabeth.

ELIZABETH. What a waste.

STEPHEN. Of what?

ELIZABETH. Of you.

STEPHEN. I'm not looking for trouble.

ELIZABETH. No?

She comes to him.

STEPHEN. No.

ELIZABETH. You never think about me? Down the years, the seasons rolling by since last time I was here?

STEPHEN. Sure.

ELIZABETH. Could I live here, do you think?

STEPHEN. You'd be too bored. No drama. No letters from the Vatican. Only trips to Sligo general hospital when Billie gets herself knocked down.

ELIZABETH. You wouldn't sell this place? Go to Dublin or somewhere?

STEPHEN *shakes his head.*

Somewhere near me?

STEPHEN. I could ask you all the same things.

ELIZABETH. That's true. Maybe that's why I feel like I know you. I never bothered with…

STEPHEN. The world?

ELIZABETH (*shrugs*). Isn't this the world?

STEPHEN. You never have dates? Nice men to buy you your dinner.

ELIZABETH. There was a nice old gentleman. His wife was sick. He took me for drives, we got coffee. But… ah, it was just all too…

STEPHEN. Sexual?

ELIZABETH (*smiles*). Sad. My mum and sisters all think I'm mad.

STEPHEN. I wonder why.

ELIZABETH. Mm. All that feminist stuff always annoyed me. I always thought the answer – for me – was something to do with men. Boys. Just the way I was. The rare creatures were the most fascinating. Look where it's led me.

STEPHEN. Hm.

ELIZABETH. I mean, everybody uses pleasure, don't they? To skate across the surface of everything. High above the horrific depths. A cup of coffee. A slice of cake, a wallop of gin or a furtive glance – that's enough to sustain your next leap across the next black crack in the ice. Then you realise no one else is going anywhere much either, just across the next little crack. And then you meet someone like Pierre. Fuck knows exactly where he's going, but fuck me, it's *somewhere*.

STEPHEN *laughs*.

What?

STEPHEN. You really have mass every day? Just you and him?

ELIZABETH. Every morning in the living room.

STEPHEN. Fucking hell.

ELIZABETH. A bit of mass would do you good!

STEPHEN. Get off.

ACT TWO   45

ELIZABETH. They're taking the house off us.

STEPHEN. What?

ELIZABETH. The church.

STEPHEN. What about them?

ELIZABETH. They're taking the house back. We've nowhere to go.

STEPHEN. Is that… is that …

ELIZABETH. Stephen.

STEPHEN. What?

FATHER PIERRE. Hello?

> ELIZABETH *freezes as* FATHER PIERRE *blindly peers into the room.*

Where is everybody?

STEPHEN. Pierre…

FATHER PIERRE. Dermot?

STEPHEN. No, it's me, Stephen.

FATHER PIERRE. Stephen?

STEPHEN (*pulling on his trousers, his shirt*). Yeah, Stephen.

FATHER PIERRE. Where's Elizabeth?

STEPHEN. Is she not with you?

FATHER PIERRE. Who's that there?

STEPHEN. Where?

FATHER PIERRE. There! Elizabeth? Elizabeth?

STEPHEN. There's nobody there.

FATHER PIERRE. What am I… [*looking at*]?

BILLIE (*coming in behind* FATHER PIERRE). Where's the pancakes?

STEPHEN. What?

BILLIE. You said you'd make pancakes.

STEPHEN. Yeah, I...

ELIZABETH slips out while FATHER PIERRE *looks at* BILLIE. BILLIE *ignores* ELIZABETH.

FATHER PIERRE. Are we having pancakes?

STEPHEN. No, here, look. There's all this grub – this is gonna be breakfast. Billie – you sort out Father Pierre, good girl. Here...

He grabs food, stuffing a sandwich in his mouth.

It's all good.

BILLIE. Can we have cake?

STEPHEN. You can have whatever you like.

FATHER PIERRE. I might just say a little prayer before we...

STEPHEN. Yeah, I'll be back in a minute. I need the toilet. I'll put the kettle on.

STEPHEN *takes his boots and his jacket out.*

BILLIE. Here, Father. Look, cake, here. Sit down.

FATHER PIERRE. Where is it?

BILLIE. It's coming. Are you going home on the train?

FATHER PIERRE. We only just got here.

BILLIE. That's irrelevant to the question I asked you.

FATHER PIERRE. No, Elizabeth drives.

BILLIE. Let her drive. Race her and I bet you'd win 'cause she'd be snarled up in Mullingar and Kinnegad.

FATHER PIERRE. I'm in no rush.

BILLIE. You're glad you've retired.

FATHER PIERRE. I'll never retire. What would I do all day? All night.

BILLIE. I'm awake all night. I think all night.

FATHER PIERRE. Think about what?

BILLIE. Statistics, times, dates, routes, places, connectivity.

ACT TWO   47

FATHER PIERRE. Okay. Why exactly?

BILLIE. I love it. Though it used to be paint.

FATHER PIERRE. What did?

BILLIE. What I thought about all night.

FATHER PIERRE. What about paint?

BILLIE. The history of paint, pigment, colours, shades, what colours make what colours when you blend them, charts, the possibility of new colours. Before that it was chimpanzees. But I was younger.

FATHER PIERRE. What was?

BILLIE. What I thought about all night. Their social structure, their habitat, their distribution in the world. The pop charts, I focus on that still – can't sleep. Get up early, before Stephen, and I go out to the chickens and I let them out of the coop. I keep them locked up at night 'cause the foxes come and try and get them.

FATHER PIERRE. Of course.

BILLIE. Then I wake Stephen up to make boiled eggs.

FATHER PIERRE. Why don't you make them?

BILLIE. I burnt my hands. And I have rheumatism already anyhow. I got knocked down in town and fell on my hands. They didn't heal well.

FATHER PIERRE. What kind of God would want you to experience that pain? Or witness it? Shall I tell you?

BILLIE. Oh, listen, if you do race Elizabeth home, the fourteen hundred from Sligo has no buffet car.

FATHER PIERRE. A connoisseur of pain. No less.

BILLIE. But there is a trolley service.

FATHER PIERRE. Do you like it here, Billie?

BILLIE. I prefer the kitchen.

FATHER PIERRE. No, I mean, living here. Wouldn't you be happier in a nice place, a nice town with a bookshop. Or a train station?

BILLIE. Which one?

FATHER PIERRE. Like anywhere.

ELIZABETH comes in with a bottle and a rag and some dressing, etc.

ELIZABETH. Alright, show me.

FATHER PIERRE. There you are. You know, I think we've had progress.

ELIZABETH helps him sit, opening his shirt so she can dress something on his back.

How is it? It's smaller, isn't it?

ELIZABETH. It's harder.

FATHER PIERRE. But it's smaller and this morning I swear I coulda swore I saw something.

ELIZABETH. No… what?

FATHER PIERRE. A deer – a little baby deer.

ELIZABETH. You weren't dreaming?

FATHER PIERRE. Sure it's all a fucking dream.

ELIZABETH. That's true.

FATHER PIERRE. Billie – would you like me to bless you?

BILLIE. Where?

FATHER PIERRE. In your mind?

BILLIE. No, I don't want to shift my thought processes.

FATHER PIERRE *(indicating* ELIZABETH*)*. You know what I say to this one here? Be free to find a path in life – not to be hiding in under my wing… What do you think?

BILLIE. Well, that's right, you're an old man. She's not old.

FATHER PIERRE. Now. And I'm back home now. I don't need anyone now.

He stands facing ELIZABETH.

ELIZABETH. Well, I'll just have to make my own way then, won't I?

FATHER PIERRE. Yes. I'm afraid you will. But that's... Celebrate! You know?

ELIZABETH. Well, whoop-de-doo.

LYDIA *comes in.*

LYDIA. Is this all still here? Was nothing put in the fridge?

BILLIE. We're eating it!

LYDIA. There's flies everywhere.

BILLIE. They need to eat too.

LYDIA. Where's Stephen?

FATHER PIERRE. Good morning...

LYDIA. Lydia.

FATHER PIERRE. Lybia.

LYDIA. Lydia.

FATHER PIERRE. Olivia.

LYDIA/BILLIE. Lydia, Lydia, Lydia, Lydia...

FATHER PIERRE. Lydia! Lydia, of course! Lydia, Lydia, Lydia...

LYDIA *takes a plastic bag from a pile of stuff in the corner and starts chucking rubbish into it.*

Is your husband here? I mean Dermot, not, em...

LYDIA. Yes, I know. Dermot. Yeah.

FATHER PIERRE. He said he'd give me a lift.

LYDIA. Oh yeah, where?

FATHER PIERRE. Into town. See the solicitor. Go to the bank.

LYDIA. Well, I can bring you if you...

FATHER PIERRE. Dermot said he'd bring me.

LYDIA. Alright. Where's Stephen?

BILLIE. Up his arse looking for potatoes.

LYDIA. Billie...

BILLIE. Can we talk about tr…

LYDIA. Not just now.

BILLIE. I'mma see if there's any eggs.

FATHER PIERRE. Lovely.

　BILLIE *goes*.

　You have a peculiar energy, Lydia.

LYDIA. You have a fairly wonky one yourself.

FATHER PIERRE. Ha ha! Yes, well, have you seen Elizabeth? I need to get dressed.

LYDIA. I saw her go into the bathroom.

FATHER PIERRE. Alright, I'll…

　STEPHEN *comes in*.

　Ah, Dermot! Good man, I'll just get dressed.

STEPHEN. No, it's Stephen.

FATHER PIERRE. Oh, Stephen. Oh well.

　FATHER PIERRE *goes*.

LYDIA (*continuing her work*). I brought you some clothes. Everything you wear looks absolutely ancient – the same with Billie. Do you never buy her anything?

STEPHEN. Who's looking at us?

LYDIA. I am! And you should. When you see yourself in the mirror. What colours are any of your clothes, even? Everything is all so faded – you and Billie are like two indeterminate grey scarecrows going about.

STEPHEN. Alright. I don't want to wear Dermot's clothes.

LYDIA. It's stuff he's never worn. And stuff there for Billie that my Mary never wore. Brand new – so no grousing. Did you get it?

　LYDIA *works furiously*.

STEPHEN. Get what?

LYDIA. The water. From the fox's covert.

STEPHEN. You that desperate?

LYDIA. I must be.

STEPHEN. Why him?

LYDIA. 'Cause when someone loves you, they show you the person no one else sees.

STEPHEN. You're sure that person is in there?

LYDIA. Yes, I believe it's…

STEPHEN. And what if it's not? If it's a hopeless case?

LYDIA (*shrugs*). Then I am too.

DERMOT (*quoting*). 'In the nineteenth chamber to behold his life, the sons of his father and his faithful wife…'

They turn to see that DERMOT *is coming in with* FREYA *and* BILLIE.

BILLIE. And his girlfriend.

DERMOT. Oof! You see that? The dagger straight in. Only siblings do that, you know.

LYDIA. Where's the bin gone?

STEPHEN *points to the hall.* LYDIA *goes.*

STEPHEN. For fuck's sake, Dermot.

DERMOT. Yeah, well, look, so you may as well know, I've moved out. Or I'm moving out.

STEPHEN. Oh okay. You've told Lydia? Like, what's…

DERMOT. She's not blind.

STEPHEN. Told your kids?

DERMOT. They wouldn't understand.

STEPHEN. Okay great. So that's…

DERMOT. Look, I'm only here to give Father Pierre a lift to his appointments – I haven't come here for… I don't need a whole… like… it's the 1980s. I've been honest with you. I'm just… like, telling you.

STEPHEN. Okay. (*To* FREYA.) And you're just... How old are you?

FREYA. What's that got to do with it?

DERMOT. Leave her out of it.

FREYA. I only know, like... my... side of... So...

STEPHEN. Okay, so why don't you all just fuck off out of it.

DERMOT (*advancing quickly*). Hey! Hey, watch your tongue.

STEPHEN. Or what?

DERMOT (*pointing at* STEPHEN*'s head*). Don't fucking make me – you never won a fight with me yet and you're not gonna now so...

STEPHEN (*seeing that* BRENDAN *is standing at the door*). Okay, great, yeah. Brendan.

BRENDAN. Is it okay if I ... get my...

STEPHEN. Your money. Oh yeah. (*Searches his pockets.*) Sure, hold on.

He finds a chequebook.

Can I write you a cheque?

BRENDAN (*shrugs*). Yeah.

DERMOT. A fuckin' cheque. I ask you.

BRENDAN, BILLIE, DERMOT *and* FREYA *stand there while* STEPHEN *tries to write a cheque with a bad pen.*

So howarya, Brendan? What's going on?

BRENDAN. Not much.

DERMOT. He has you doin' all the knick-knacks.

BRENDAN. Yeah, I don't mind.

DERMOT. Does your ma not need you?

BRENDAN. I'm only over the way. I don't mind. I can pop over here.

DERMOT. Few extra shillings.

BRENDAN. Mm.

DERMOT. How much does he pay you? Personal question. Fuck-all is the personal answer. Yeah. Tell your folks I said hello. I'll get Pierre. (*Calls out.*) Pierre! Where are ya? (*To* BILLIE.) Billie, come here.

BILLIE. What?

DERMOT. Give me a hug.

BILLIE. No.

DERMOT. Come on!

BILLIE. No!

DERMOT. She'd never give you a hug. Come on. Show me you love me.

BILLIE. No.

DERMOT (*reaching to hold her*). Show me you love me.

BILLIE. No! Get off me! Get off!

She hits at him.

DERMOT. You see? I love you anyway. (*Calling out.*) Pierre! Where are ya?

FATHER PIERRE (*off*). What?

DERMOT. Are you 'right?

FATHER PIERRE (*off*). What? Yeah.

STEPHEN. I need a pen. Youse don't have a pen? This fucking...

BRENDAN. No, sorry.

STEPHEN. Just a sec.

STEPHEN *goes.* FREYA, BILLIE *and* BRENDAN *stand there.*

FREYA. Hiya, Brendan.

BRENDAN. Hiya.

FREYA. Do you not remember me?

BRENDAN. I do, yeah. You live over the other side of Cill
Srianán.

FREYA. Yeah. You used always wave at me in the mornings.
And I'd see you bringing the cows down in the evening.

BRENDAN. Yeah, yeah, I know. You have a sister.

BILLIE. You have a sister?

FREYA. Yeah. And our ma – and Dermot now. He stays over.

BILLIE. This is mad!

FREYA. I know.

FREYA *shrugs*.

BRENDAN. What does your ma say?

FREYA. She's in the hospital in Ballinasloe.

BRENDAN. Oh okay.

FREYA. Yeah. Her nerves. Drink. The drink was for her nerves.

BRENDAN. Yeah, that's…

FREYA. Suddenly you don't know us!

BRENDAN. No!

FREYA. Are you saying you didn't see my ma drinking in your
pub up there – you didn't serve her. She's the only woman
ever in the place.

BRENDAN. Yeah, well, my ma serves in the bar more than me.

FREYA. Yeah, well, anyway she can't afford the pub this long
time.

BILLIE. So what does she do?

FREYA. Drink at home. Lemonade bottles with vodka in them.
Poitín in 'em.

BILLIE. Your pub is only ever lonely old men anyhow.

BRENDAN. Mm. Well, local people, yeah.

BILLIE. Middle-of-nowhere people.

FREYA. My ma used to meet fellas in there sometimes. Little wiry fellas always. Denim jackets, roll-up fags. I'd get up out of bed, there'd be some fucking eejit in our kitchen. Always gobshites. Laughing then crying – rows all the time.

BRENDAN. It's not all that bad. You should come in some time.

BILLIE. We could all go. Bring your sister. They're getting Pac-Man.

BRENDAN. No, we're not any more.

BILLIE. I thought you were getting a Pac-Man machine.

BRENDAN. My mam said no.

BILLIE. You should get a pool table.

BRENDAN. Too small for a pool table.

BILLIE. Get a snooker table.

BRENDAN. Anyway, yeah, come in, bring your sister. I'll give you a free 7-Up.

FREYA. My sister's not home either.

BRENDAN. Oh okay.

BILLIE. Where's she gone? She get the...?

FREYA. Nah she's... I don't know where she is. Yeah. My mum said I wasn't a good sister any more so...

BRENDAN. Oh.

FREYA. Yeah. Said I'd 'changed'. The doctor had her sectioned 'cause she kept going on about it. Then my sister was too sick to go to school or work.

BRENDAN. Sorry to hear that.

FREYA. Do you like going for walks?

BRENDAN. I do a lotta walking anyway.

FREYA. Walking the cows all around.

BRENDAN. Yeah.

BILLIE (*to* FREYA). What are your dreams then?

FREYA. What do you mean?

BILLIE. You gonna marry Uncle Dermot, get all his cafés and shops?

FREYA. No, I dunno. What are you gonna do? (*To* BRENDAN.) Or you? Just become your dad – running the pub and the farm?

BRENDAN. Yeah, become my mum and my dad. I already am. Well, maybe not my dad.

FREYA. Why? Is he not very cool?

BRENDAN. Nah, he's not very… alive.

FREYA. Oh.

BILLIE. His mum is a very holy woman.

FREYA. Yeah?

BRENDAN. What? Well, like – yeah – she goes to mass. So does everybody.

FREYA. She probably says the rosary, does she?

BRENDAN (*laughs*). Mm. Every night.

FREYA. Do you say it too?

BRENDAN. Mm.

FREYA. With your mum?

BRENDAN. Mm.

FREYA. Why?

BRENDAN. Dunno, just do.

BILLIE. What do you want?

FREYA. Nothing.

BILLIE. Where are you going?

FREYA. Nowhere.

BILLIE. Nothing Nowhere Nohow – that's what they should call you. Fucking nowhere.

LYDIA (*coming through*). Come here, Billie, I have a few things for you to try on.

BILLIE. Where?

LYDIA. In your room.

BILLIE. Nah, I'm alright.

LYDIA. Come on we can talk about cartography.

BILLIE. You talk.

LYDIA. I will.

> LYDIA *goes.* BILLIE *looks at* BRENDAN, *then follows* LYDIA *out.*

FREYA. I know you like me.

> BRENDAN *looks at her.*

You don't have to say anything.

> DERMOT *comes in.*

DERMOT. You know each other?

FREYA. No. Do you have fags in the car?

DERMOT. Yeah, I think so. It's not locked.

> LYDIA *comes in to pick up another bag of clothes.* FREYA *goes out.* BRENDAN *stands there while* LYDIA *looks through the bag and finds a jacket.*

Yak-a-doodle-doo, ha?

BRENDAN. What?

DERMOT. I said yak-a-doodle-doo.

BRENDAN. Mm. I'll…

DERMOT. Yeah, see ya. Say hello to your ma.

> BRENDAN *goes.*

How are the kids?

LYDIA. They're alright.

DERMOT. I'm gonna take them for a meal.

LYDIA. Yeah, they told me.

DERMOT. Look, it's better they're out of the way of all the fighting and the...

LYDIA. Yeah. I wasn't fighting. I didn't want to fight.

DERMOT. Neither did I – (*With suppressed fury.*) But I have to be able to fucking live, Lydia.

LYDIA. I never would have stopped you.

DERMOT. I can't go around living like I'm in some kind of freaking comedy! Like I'm in the wrong life!

LYDIA. So tell me. What?!

DERMOT. It's not – it's like there's two roads – one is all blocked and the other one just takes you to the moon – it's a no-brainer.

LYDIA. I'm not blocking you doing anything.

DERMOT. It's not a physical block! Did I say that? It's, how can I say it. It's like I can't live – like if I go down that road I'm gonna fucking die. Do you not know how freaking scary that is?

LYDIA. Can you come home and ask Dr Kilgallon for...

DERMOT. I'm already on the pills Kilgallon gave me. I'm on them!

LYDIA. And drinking on top of them.

DERMOT. Yes! 'Cause I'm trying to figure myself out here. For me. For once.

LYDIA. Doesn't seem like I have much choice.

DERMOT. Ah, don't be so pathetic.

LYDIA. I'm pathetic. Is that what you think?

DERMOT. Most wives would lose their fucking nut and rip my freaking eyes out.

LYDIA. I love ya. What can I say? I love you.

DERMOT. But I don't even know what that fucking means!! Can't you not fucking see that??

LYDIA. So you're not in love with this... this...

DERMOT. Freya.

LYDIA. Freya...

DERMOT. I'm trying to explain it. I'm under some... it's mad... – but that's – it's where I have to go. I'm... (*Changes tack.*) I'm gonna bring the kids out for an omelette. And chips. And look, listen, I'm not... I do care about you – of course I do, and that's why I want you to consider... this... for yourself too.

LYDIA. Consider what?

DERMOT. This... To find someone who can...

LYDIA. No.

DERMOT. Why not?

LYDIA. Because I love you. It's never changed. I still...

DERMOT. But that's not normal – after all these years! Do you not see that?

LYDIA *nods*.

Do you not see it?

LYDIA *nods*.

(*Laughs.*) Like, that's mad! Do you not see?

LYDIA. I do.

DERMOT. Yeah!

FATHER PIERRE *comes in.* LYDIA *goes so* PIERRE *won't know she's upset.*

FATHER PIERRE. I'm ready for the fields of battle!

DERMOT. Good man. You 'right?

FATHER PIERRE. Good to go. Lots to discuss. I want to go to the bank – my solicitor...

DERMOT. Yeah?

FATHER PIERRE. I'd like to... How are you?

DERMOT. How am I?

FATHER PIERRE. Yeah.

DERMOT. I'm – I'm actually very good. It's the circumstances around me that are…

FATHER PIERRE. I can feel it.

DERMOT. Yeah?

FATHER PIERRE. I can see it. Would you like to make your confession?

DERMOT. What? Now?

FATHER PIERRE. Yes – in the car – on our way.

DERMOT. No.

FATHER PIERRE. Come here.

FATHER PIERRE holds DERMOT's hand. FREYA steps in the doorway, watching them.

God understands.

DERMOT. Really?

FATHER PIERRE. Oh yes. Of course he does. I can feel your suffering and I'm going to help you and support you. So will you rely on me?

DERMOT. I will yeah.

FATHER PIERRE. Will you depend upon me?

DERMOT. Yes.

DERMOT looks up to see that FREYA has been standing there, watching.

Now! There we go.

ELIZABETH *comes in.*

ELIZABETH. Did you have your breakfast?

FATHER PIERRE. I did, I'm good to go.

LYDIA *comes in with* BILLIE.

DERMOT. Yup – so we'll be off to do the errands – do youse need anything here?

BILLIE. We don't need eggs.

ELIZABETH. Anything else?

BILLIE. Just goodies.

DERMOT. Billie, give Father Pierre his stick there.

BILLIE. He has it.

DERMOT (*to* LYDIA). I'll, eh...

FATHER PIERRE. Are we right? For the Big Apple.

ELIZABETH. Big day out.

DERMOT, FATHER PIERRE, FREYA *and* ELIZABETH *head out.* BILLIE *watches at the window, then also goes out.*

LYDIA *is alone.* STEPHEN *comes in. He watches* LYDIA *for a moment. He comes to her with a small bottle of water and gives it to her.*

LYDIA. I didn't think there'd be muck in it.

STEPHEN. Dermot used to eat muck when we were kids. He ate it with a spoon. You give it to him in milk. No alcohol. And when he sleeps you need to be the first person he sees. When he wakes up.

LYDIA *nods and sits despondently.*

Although, I was you, I'd just let him...

LYDIA (*interrupting him*). Yeah, I know what you'd do, you told me.

LYDIA *gets up and fetches cash from her bag.*

STEPHEN. Thanks.

BILLIE *comes in.*

Good luck with the...

LYDIA *nods.* STEPHEN *goes out.*

BILLIE. You alright?

BILLIE *plays the piano.*

LYDIA. Mm.

BILLIE. You sure?

LYDIA *nods*.

You look like you need a hug.

LYDIA. No, I'm alright.

BILLIE *plays the piano*.

ELIZABETH *comes in*.

BILLIE *sings 'A Heart Needs a Home' by Richard & Linda Thompson.*

LYDIA *sits, looking out, holding the bottle. She looks down at it.*

Lights.

ACT THREE

It's evening. The sun is about to set, low-angled evening light cuts through the room. The sun gradually sets during the act, fading to darkness.

Some chairs are dotted about the room, including two shabby-looking deckchairs brought in from a shed. STEPHEN *and* LYDIA *sit in these while* BILLIE *stands at the piano, picking out a spare tune. She tries it on the higher keys, then tries it on the bass notes.*

STEPHEN. Fragilysis.

LYDIA. Fra...?

STEPHEN. Fragilysis.

LYDIA. Sounds real.

BILLIE. Fragilysis... Fragilysis...

LYDIA. Like fragile?

STEPHEN. It's like fragile. The word is like fragile, but it means something very different.

LYDIA. It's made-up.

BILLIE. How do you know?

LYDIA. I know by his face.

BILLIE. How?

LYDIA. By looking at his face! I can see. He's having us on.

STEPHEN. Fragilysis.

LYDIA. It's not a word.

BILLIE. What does it mean?

STEPHEN. It means when something is right on the edge – you know, in a state of...

BILLIE. Falling-off.

STEPHEN. Yeah, like imminent... demise... a state of...

LYDIA. Fragilysis.

STEPHEN. Yeah, fragilysis.

LYDIA. Look – he's actually laughing.

STEPHEN. I'm not! Look it up.

LYDIA. No way – that's a point to me. It's not a word. He's trying to not smile.

STEPHEN. I'm not smiling – it's my natural, this is my...

BILLIE. He's in a state of fragilysis.

LYDIA. He is in my backside. It's not a word, right?

STEPHEN. It's not a word.

LYDIA. I knew it.

BILLIE. It's a good one though.

LYDIA. I have one – Predonitial.

BILLIE. Predon-eye-is.

LYDIA. No, predonitial.

BILLIE. Ishill...

LYDIA. Something that has to happen before something else can happen.

BILLIE. It's predonitial that some gas escapes before full evacuation.

LYDIA. Exactly.

STEPHEN. Predonitial. Predonitial. 'It was predonitial...' (*Shrugs.*) 'It's predonitional.'

LYDIA. No. Predonitial. Not predonitional. 'It was predonitial.'

ELIZABETH *comes in*.

ELIZABETH. Hello.

LYDIA. Hello.

ELIZABETH. Are we early?

LYDIA. We must be.

BILLIE. I don't want to sit through mass.

ELIZABETH. I don't think he's going to say mass. He said mass this afternoon in his bedroom. I think this evening is just – he wants us to gather.

BILLIE. To say goodbye?

ELIZABETH. I don't think so.

BILLIE. Talk about rail networks?

ELIZABETH. Probably not.

ELIZABETH *wanders to the window.*

No, his mood feels very…

BILLIE. Relaxed?

ELIZABETH. Subdued.

BILLIE. We're all subdued, bitch.

ELIZABETH. I beg your pardon?

LYDIA. Billie was upset.

ELIZABETH. Oh?

LYDIA. A fox got into her chickens.

ELIZABETH. Oh no.

BILLIE. I said I don't want to talk about it.

LYDIA. Sorry.

STEPHEN. You left the coop open.

BILLIE. I have never left the coop open.

ELIZABETH. Are they… Were they…?

BILLIE. They're all dead, okay?

ELIZABETH. Oh no. I'm so sorry.

LYDIA. And nobody heard anything?

ELIZABETH. I didn't.

BILLIE. Silent death stalks the land.

ELIZABETH. I'm sorry, Billie.

BILLIE. Yeah, I know, you've said that about eleven times.

LYDIA. Billie, Elizabeth's only being nice.

BILLIE. I didn't say she isn't. Don't worry about it, Elizabeth. It's just the cycle of nature. You have to learn from it.

ELIZABETH. Mm.

BILLIE. You can learn from the fox. Two types of people in the world, Elizabeth. The fox and the prize heifer. Which one are you?

ELIZABETH. Well, I hope I'm not the second one.

BILLIE. Yeah, well, hoping won't save you – you need to decide. What do you want to be – the prize heifer stands there on fair day, tied to a pole where everyone can look at her, walk around her – no mystery, you can walk all around, even look up her arsehole if you want.

LYDIA. Billie!

BILLIE. Well, you can. Twiddle her bits. She won't do nothing. So do you want to be the prize heifer, standing there like a dunce in the broad daylight, or do you wanna be the fox – only coming out at night, scavenging in people's bins, causing trouble and being unknown.

ELIZABETH. Well... I don't know, I don't want to scavenge in anyone's bin.

BILLIE. We're using metaphor.

ELIZABETH. A what?

BILLIE. Just... remain in the realm of metaphor for five minutes of your bleeding life, will you?

ELIZABETH laughs.

ELIZABETH. I'll try!

BILLIE. I'm tryna teach you something.

ACT THREE   67

ELIZABETH. I'll be the fox then. I am a fox. Like you.

BILLIE. You probably are!

ELIZABETH. How are you, Stephen?

STEPHEN. What? Yeah, I'm…

He's not engaging with ELIZABETH. *She gets it.*

ELIZABETH. Hey, I have a word. What's the opposite of nostalgia?

BILLIE. Neuralgia.

ELIZABETH. Neuralgia, yeah, for windowsills and radiators and scrunching down under the net curtains and hiding at Christmas.

BILLIE. Yeah, that'd give you serious neuralgia.

LYDIA. Oh, play something together, will you? Stephen, play something with Billie.

STEPHEN. Play what?

LYDIA. Something together.

ELIZABETH. You play together?

STEPHEN. I can't play.

BILLIE. He can.

STEPHEN. I haven't played in years.

ELIZABETH. Play something!

LYDIA. Play something together.

ELIZABETH. Yes, go on!

ELIZABETH grabs STEPHEN by the sleeve. LYDIA takes the other arm. They pull him out of his deckchair and over to the piano.

STEPHEN. I can't play. Leave me alone.

BILLIE. You can.

LYDIA. He can.

STEPHEN. Stop it! Leave me alone!

He pulls away.

LYDIA (*shaking her wrist*). Alright. Jaysus, Stephen. We're only messing.

STEPHEN. Yeah, no, it's just...

LYDIA. What?

BILLIE. Stephen.

STEPHEN (*relents*). Here, come on. Play the...

BILLIE. The what? The...

She plays the chords for 'Pavane pour une infante défunte' by Maurice Ravel.

STEPHEN. Yeah.

STEPHEN *comes and plays along with* BILLIE, *accompanied by their laughs and comments to each other as they make mistakes or start a bit over, skipping parts and finding their way repeatedly to the signature melody. But this is interrupted after a few moments by the sound of a handbell ringing from somewhere in the house.*

ELIZABETH. That's Pierre. He'll need help getting dressed.

She starts to go but sees something outside.

(*Going.*) Billie, your young gentleman is outside.

She goes.

BILLIE (*going to window*). Who?

LYDIA. It's Brendan.

BILLIE. He's not my gentleman.

LYDIA. Was he invited too?

STEPHEN. He wouldn't miss a mass.

LYDIA. Go out to him, Billie.

BILLIE. Why?

LYDIA. It's raining.

BILLIE. He's used to it.

LYDIA. Have you no pity? He looks sick in his heart.

BILLIE. Well, I can't cure him.

STEPHEN. Billie, don't leave him out there.

BILLIE (*going*). For Jaysus's sake, can he not not just knock at the door, no?

LYDIA. Evidently not.

> LYDIA *and* STEPHEN *are alone. They are quiet for a moment. She glances at him; he appears preoccupied.*

So here. You owe me money.

STEPHEN. What money?

LYDIA. Five hundred pounds.

STEPHEN. I don't owe you five hundred pounds.

LYDIA. Don't come the gom with me, you filled up a jam jar with tap water, scooped a spoonful of muck in it...

STEPHEN. Aw, here we go...

LYDIA. ...And told me you got it from the well.

STEPHEN. I did! I got it from the well. Look at my bleeding hands! I nearly tore the arse out of myself going in through the hawthorn.

LYDIA. That's bullshit, Stephen! I know you, I know your brother – I've lived with him my whole adult life! And your sister – out there now punishing that poor young fella youse both exploit...

STEPHEN. What?!

LYDIA. You're all liars you all treat everyone the same.

STEPHEN. Ah, go fuck yourself, Lydia, I did what you asked me, I'll give you your money back if you want it.

LYDIA. Yeah, well, I do.

STEPHEN. I don't have it on me now!

LYDIA. Aw yeah, course you don't, why would I expect anything different from a McFaddin. You're all the fucking same.

STEPHEN. I'll get you your money – whatcha wanna bother coming up here for then any more? Who minds your children?

LYDIA. What?

STEPHEN. You're never out of this place, what are you doing up here? I know my brother's not minding them!

LYDIA. They're old enough.

STEPHEN. How old are they? Ten?

LYDIA. Eleven! The little one is nine – but she's actually more mature than the older fella – they look after themselves anyway – they're like their father – they don't need me, and they make it very plain.

STEPHEN. Yeah, I wonder why.

LYDIA *stands looking out the window.*

Did you give it to him like I told ya? Just before he went to sleep?

LYDIA. He came to see the kids. Read to them in bed. Came down the stairs sheepishly. He was guilty. I gave him whiskey. I had it in. Gave it to him, listened to him moaning and wailing, till he could hardly stand – that girl, she drives him mad, you know – then gave him the water with the muck in it. He slept on the couch.

STEPHEN. And you were the first person he saw when he woke up.

LYDIA. Yeah, I sat there all night.

STEPHEN (*exasperated/exhausted by the whole situation*). Fucking hell…

LYDIA. He snored and snored and dreaming. Talking to himself. Nightmares. The whole lot. Then, finally, he opened his eyes, looked right at me.

STEPHEN. And?

LYDIA. He just went, got sick in the little toilet under the stairs. I gave him a drink – of the water.

STEPHEN. You gave it to him again?

LYDIA. Yeah.

STEPHEN. And?

LYDIA. He threw up again – there was all muck in it, Stephen. And he left.

STEPHEN. Well, I don't know.

LYDIA. Yeah, well, like everything else in life, it's all just a legend, an illusion.

STEPHEN. Mm.

They are quiet for a moment.

LYDIA. What am I gonna do?

STEPHEN. It does work. I've seen it working.

LYDIA. On who?

STEPHEN. On you.

LYDIA. Me?

STEPHEN. Why do you think you're so lost?

LYDIA. What do you…?

STEPHEN. Look at it.

LYDIA. He gave me the water?

STEPHEN. I gave it to you.

LYDIA. When?

STEPHEN. When we were fifteen. When you stayed here when your dad was in hospital and your auntie used to bring you up here and we'd have bonfires that summer.

LYDIA. Yeah?

STEPHEN. I was mad about ya. I was a kid.

LYDIA. What did you…

STEPHEN. I didn't mean anything. It was… I mean it was all only a superstition. I got some water from the spring. Put it in a little plastic holy-water bottle. It was easier to get at back then – or maybe I was just smaller. Squeezing in through all the thorns back then and you'd find yourself in a little, like a chamber of branches with the light sparkling and there it was, this little stream up there, a tiny waterfall pouring out of nowhere. You were staying the night with us, so I… I put it on your Rice Krispies when we were all having our supper. You ate it, and I set my alarm 'cause I was gonna be the first person you saw when you woke up. I never slept all night. But I must have dropped off before it got bright. I woke up before the alarm – but… Dermot had already snuck into your room, do you remember?

LYDIA. Stephen…

STEPHEN. Youse never even saw me. I crept down the landing and I pushed the door a tiny creak, but he was already in there. He'd snuck in and he was kneeling beside your bed and I could hear the two a youse laughing and talking and…

LYDIA. Stephen…

STEPHEN. He never even had to try…! I'd done it all for him.

LYDIA. You fucking…

She comes to STEPHEN *and starts thumping him with her fists.*

You fucking did this to me!

STEPHEN. I'm sorry! I'm sorry, alright?

FREYA *comes in.* LYDIA *goes.*

(*Taking it out on* FREYA.) What the fuck are you doing? Who are you anyway? You're causing fucking mayhem!

FREYA. That's your despair and anger. It's not mine. I didn't cause it. That's your own situation here.

STEPHEN. What would you know about anybody's situation?

FREYA (*undaunted*). 'Cause Dermot talks to me. He tells me. I see you up here – a grown man living with his own sister. You know what that looks like? It looks sad.

STEPHEN. I look sad.

FREYA. Yes, anybody would say that.

STEPHEN. So I'm sad. So what? You don't think you look sad? You know what you look like? You look like a little witch.

FREYA. Yeah, maybe I am. I don't care.

STEPHEN. Well, maybe you should.

FREYA. And maybe you should too.

STEPHEN. Should what?

FREYA. Care.

STEPHEN. Ah, leave me alone, will ya? Leave us all alone. What's wrong with finding a fella your own age, for fuck's sake?

FREYA. He is my age. Like you're my age.

STEPHEN. Well, I'm not.

FREYA. Says who?

STEPHEN. The laws of time.

FREYA. I don't think you understand time either. What if I'd found you first? Out here on your own in the dark.

STEPHEN. What?

FREYA (*gently mocking him*). 'What?'… 'What?'

They stand there. She comes closer. He looks at her. She lifts her face to his, for a moment anything might happen…

STEPHEN *raises his eyes to see* ELIZABETH *standing in the doorway.*

ELIZABETH. Hello.

STEPHEN. Hello. What's happening?

ELIZABETH. Nothing. I mean, where is everybody?

STEPHEN. Yeah, I dunno.

The three of them stand there awkwardly for a moment.

He's not, eh… saying mass or…?

ELIZABETH. No, he just said he wanted us all to gather. (*To* FREYA.) Hello.

FREYA. I like your skirt.

ELIZABETH. Thank you. I like your pants. I like your hair.

FREYA. Yeah.

FATHER PIERRE (*finding his way in*). Aha, aha! Lost followers of the Roman Church.

FREYA. I don't follow the Roman Church. It follows me.

FATHER PIERRE. We may as well the way we're going! So what do you believe?

FREYA. Me? I believe something I once read on the back of a cracker. That this – (*Indicates 'everything'.*) is all a shrug from a sleeping mind.

FATHER PIERRE. Whose sleeping mind?

FREYA. Well, God, of course. God's asleep – and we are the dream. And when God wakes, all of this will blow away and everything will cease because the only perfection is nothingness. And what is God if not perfection? It said on this cracker that when God wakes from this aberration he'll weep into the mercy of the void. We just guard him while he sleeps.

FATHER PIERRE. Guard him from what?

FREYA. Bad dreams. I read it in a cracker. You won't remember anything I just said.

FATHER PIERRE (*a little laugh*). Who are you exactly?

DERMOT (*coming in with a bottle of Bushmills and glasses*). Now! There we are! There he is! How's it going, Stephen? Still looking after number one?

STEPHEN. Well, someone's gotta.

DERMOT. Now. Yup. Take care of numero uno, whatever you do! Howarya, Elizabeth?

ELIZABETH. I'm fine, thank you.

DERMOT (*to* FREYA). Where were you?

FREYA. I was here.

FATHER PIERRE. Now, ha ha! Are we all gathered? What were we talking about?

DERMOT. You're not saying mass, are ya? I mean I don't mind, only I have to...

He looks at his watch.

FATHER PIERRE. No, I've said mass, no this evening is just, it's a special... I just wanted to, who's here?

DERMOT *is banging on the window.*

DERMOT (*calls*). Get in! Billie's out there with that amadán you have minding the cows.

FATHER PIERRE. Who's here?

ELIZABETH. Stephen is here and Dermot and...

FREYA. Freya.

LYDIA *comes in.*

ELIZABETH. And Freya and here's Lydia.

FATHER PIERRE. Lydia.

DERMOT (*to* LYDIA). Are the kids here?

LYDIA *shakes her head.*

Who's with them?

LYDIA. What do you care?

ELIZABETH. And Billie's coming now. Here's Billie.

FATHER PIERRE. Are we all gathered?

ELIZABETH. Yes.

BILLIE *comes in with* BRENDAN.

FATHER PIERRE. Please help yourselves. Are we gathered?

STEPHEN. Here, I have to...

He starts to go. DERMOT *and* ELIZABETH *stop him.*

DERMOT. Just let him have his spake!

ELIZABETH. This concerns you too, Stephen. Be the host.

DERMOT. Come on, hold up. Where do you have to be? Jaysus.

STEPHEN *relents*.

FATHER PIERRE. I stand here in this room and once again I'm a young boy, remembering the horseplay and the messing that went on in here. Our mother imploring us to stop. Myself and my brother desperately wrestling on the floor with our father. Our father egging us on to greater glory. I was as surprised as anyone when the Virgin Mary appeared to me out there by the hedges down at the covert to tell me I had a vocation. But there it was. I beheld the goddess, as I thought then, and I came back up here, carrying my secret thoughts in my mind like a wounded bird, and I nursed those thoughts and I dreamed of the Virgin, until I went to the priests in school to tell them my decision to join the priesthood. My father went absolutely berserk and put his hand through the window out there in the kitchen door! But I look back now, and I forgive him. I understand now what I could never had understood then, for how could I have known my vocation was indeed a higher calling than anyone before me?

As soon as I entered the seminary, I was marked for bigger things – perhaps even at the Vatican – at one time – oh yes, they flew me out there, led me round their hallowed hallways – pointed out all the massive paintings and statues to me – but of course, their forces had already gathered against me. Because they sensed the danger in my mind. They were only courting me because they knew I was on to them. Before I even quite knew it myself! No, they sent me off, all the years I laboured in the wilderness around Dundalk, in cold churches in housing estates without even a bus stop. I conscientiously administered my mission, of course, while all the while I studied and cogitated and fought and rowed with the bishop's inferior intellect until, Elizabeth will tell you, they decreed that I should no longer administer the last rites to parishioners.

Admittedly, this was clever on their part – because it was indeed during the intimacies of the last rites that I first glimpsed the entire truth.

Watching someone die – the energy it takes a person to die, the power they must summon within themselves to leave is truly awe-inspiring.

What are they clinging to exactly? Life? Surely, by the end, life has become too painful and frightening. Why not fall into the embrace of heaven? The release? And yet no – every soul resists it!! Why? Shall I tell you? Because nobody goes to heaven!

Nobody is saved, my friends. Every single one of us is destined for eternal damnation, I'm afraid.

BRENDAN. What?

FATHER PIERRE. Yes. I'm sorry to say it. What benevolent God would create this crucible of suffering we call human life? Only an evil, all-powerful psychopath who has made us his playthings.

LYDIA. So there's no God.

FATHER PIERRE. An evil god if you want to still call him a god. But he's really the kind of opposite of God. There is only a devil, my friends!

DERMOT. Well, that's not good.

FATHER PIERRE. Tell me about it. And the Church for whom I have laboured my whole life is his infernal instrument! Yes! For the illusion of hope for salvation makes our suffering all the more acute and our suffering makes his sadistic pleasure all the more satisfying. Look at the world and tell me if that doesn't make sense.

BILLIE. Yeah, makes sense.

FATHER PIERRE. Yes! So I took my findings to the powers that be – like a fucking eejit! And explained to them that this realisation – that there *is* no God only a devil – is precisely what we should be teaching because this realisation, this awareness is itself the beginning of an awakening consciousness – this is the beginning – this – is, in fact, Genesis!! This awakening within me is at last, well, the birth of God.

BILLIE. So you're God?

FATHER PIERRE. Yes.

BILLIE. *God* God?

FATHER PIERRE. I'm the beginning of God, yes. So what do the lords and masters of the Vatican – who I realise now are just the ignorant minions of the dark one – what do they do?

BILLIE. They fucking sack you.

FATHER PIERRE. Yes. Sadly. Just at the moment we need to spread this message – and to begin the fight – what do they do?

BILLIE. They cut your balls off.

FATHER PIERRE. Well, I mean, yes, but all this is by the by. So look, this brings me to the important part of the evening. I have, with the help of Dermot and Elizabeth and… I've been meeting with our solicitor and the bank and looking back at my mother's will, written under, it turns out, very peculiar circumstances where everything was left to my father. It appears another will in the form of a letter deposited by my mother in a safety deposit box in Sligo has emerged, and fortunately casts light on the entire provenance of the house, which it now appears could not have been left to you, Stephen, and Dermot and Billie, because it had, in fact, already been left to myself and my brother, your father. So, it was already half mine you see? Your father had no right to leave it to you, because he only ever owned half of it. And I've discussed it with Dermot and we've come to an understanding that my fifty per cent plus his sixteen-point-six-six-six-six per cent – if you divide my brother's half by three – you all only own sixteen-point-six-six-six per cent – and if that's added to my fifty per cent, gives us, myself and Dermot – an accumulated sixty-six-point-six-six-six-six per cent stake of ownership and as the majority owners we have decided, well, Dermot has assisted me in deciding this house shall now become a centre of retreat where disciples of our new understanding might gather their strength for the great awakening.

STEPHEN. The great what?

DERMOT. Great awakening.

FATHER PIERRE. A place of quietude, replenishment, spiritual succor. I really mean a kind fortress – or a kind of manger even – for the new nativity – the real birth of our saviour – in the heart of our new ideas.

STEPHEN. No yeah, I get all that about the devil and all that – I mean about the point-six-six-six per cent and all of that.

FATHER PIERRE. Oh, the letter! Yes, so, here we go. (*Unfolding a ragged-looking piece of paper.*) I can't read it.

DERMOT. Dad really was a… You'd have to watch him like a hawk.

FATHER PIERRE. My mother knew what he was up to, so she wrote a letter confirming he wasn't actually legally entitled to leave it to any of you! Isn't that hilarious?

STEPHEN. Great… You're coming to live here.

FATHER PIERRE. Who 'lives' anywhere? No one really 'lives' in this purgatorial…

ELIZABETH. Yes. Stephen. Yes, he, we… we'll be living here.

STEPHEN. With us?

DERMOT. In his portion, and along with mine and Billie's, and Pierre's. You can decide what you… with your…

STEPHEN. My portion?

DERMOT. Yes, you can…

STEPHEN. Live in my portion.

FATHER PIERRE. If that's what you…

STEPHEN. I don't want to live here with you.

FATHER PIERRE. Absolutely! These outhouses out the back I always thought would make beautiful cells like the old monks might use –

DERMOT. Studio apartments.

FATHER PIERRE. Yes, that's what I mean. I'm telling you, one of those – one for you, one for Billie, I'd be more than happy to look at renovations.

STEPHEN. What – live out there in the shed?

DERMOT. They wouldn't *be* sheds.

STEPHEN. With what – with this mad bollocks and a load of old fucking priests in here? (*To* DERMOT.) And what do you... Why are you even, fucking...

DERMOT. Dad shouldna left it to us, it wasn't his to leave to us – it belonged to both him and Pierre, the solicitor is appealing the deeds.

STEPHEN. What do you mean – 'appealing the deeds'? Where am I supposed to go? Where's Billie supposed to live?

FATHER PIERRE. Here! You'll live here!

STEPHEN. With a load of of mad priests?

FATHER PIERRE. And nuns.

DERMOT. Or sell your stake.

STEPHEN. To who?

DERMOT. I'll buy it.

STEPHEN. For how much?

DERMOT. We can negotiate – You know I'll look after you.

STEPHEN. You will in your shite.

DERMOT. Then stay here. Do what you want. Except just face the facts.

BILLIE. They've already done it.

STEPHEN. Done what?

BILLIE. I heard them. They've already done it.

STEPHEN. What do you mean?

BILLIE. I know they have. They were in the kitchen. They thought I was asleep.

DERMOT. Billie. For fuck's sake. (*To* STEPHEN.) The solicitor is writing to you.

STEPHEN. About what. (*To* BILLIE.) What did you hear?

DERMOT. She didn't hear anything.

BILLIE. I heard you and Pierre. Youse already signed things.

DERMOT. She doesn't know. She doesn't understand.

BILLIE. I heard youse.

FATHER PIERRE. I wanted to say something. It's important, we don't need solicitors and…

STEPHEN. What didn't she hear?

BILLIE. They're putting us out.

DERMOT. We're not! No one's putting anyone out!

STEPHEN. You're some fucking prick.

DERMOT. What would she know?! She's fucking deaf!

BILLIE. I'm not deaf! I have arthritis.

DERMOT. Well, whatever the fuck you have – she doesn't know what she heard.

BILLIE. I do.

STEPHEN. I'd believe her before I believe you.

DERMOT. Course you would, you're like trying to talk to a brick fucking wall.

STEPHEN. Yeah, I'm so inconvenient really – I know what you're up to – you're duping him as much as you're duping us and you're duping him. You'll clear us out, use his claim to do that, and then when he's popped his clogs, we'll all be gone and you'll swoop in.

DERMOT. Stephen, it's just business. It's just pieces of paper. Just accept it and live with it.

STEPHEN. Yeah, I'll live with it, like I've lived with this fucking 'Can we talk about paint?' 'Can we talk about chimpanzees?' 'Can we talk about painted chimpanzees?' Till I think my fucking head is gonna fall off. Carrying Mum up and down the stairs before she died 'cause you wouldn't put a fucking downstairs jacks in.

DERMOT. Me put a downstairs jacks in? Why didn't you put a downstairs jacks in?

STEPHEN. 'Cause I've no money 'cause I've been stuck minding Billie and stuck here with Ma till she died and you were nowhere to be found.

BILLIE. Nobody needs to mind me.

DERMOT (*to* STEPHEN, *dismissively*). Ah, would ya [*fuck off*]... Yeah, you made a great job minding Billie. Sorry, how many times has she been knocked down again?

BILLIE. Three times.

DERMOT. Three times! Where the fuck were you while she was wandering up and down the Quay Road getting knocked down by lorries? You were up here in the kitchen knocking back six-packs with the money I give youse.

STEPHEN. Money you give us? When did you ever give us money?

DERMOT. The money I give Billie – every bleeding month – every week!

STEPHEN. What money?

BILLIE. Yeah. I was gonna tell you.

STEPHEN. What money?

BILLIE. It was money for when I needed to go into town.

DERMOT. This is classic – the fucking pair a youse – two fucking gobdaws.

ELIZABETH. You're in a war, Stephen.

STEPHEN. Yeah. What?

ELIZABETH. A war, you know what a war is – you're in a war.

STEPHEN. What war?

ELIZABETH. A war like any of all the ordinary wars we're all always in. Where everybody has given up talking – and it's trial by combat – and any doubt you have lets the enemy in and proves you were wrong. And whatever it is you seem to believe in, Stephen, it has not prevailed, alright?

ACT THREE 83

FATHER PIERRE. Yes, alright, Elizabeth.

ELIZABETH. And all those closest to you – who had hopes for you – and who might have protected you, they no longer trust you. So you have no allies – and you're on your own – and you're... you're losing the war.

STEPHEN. Good! That's what I want.

ELIZABETH. Well, good – because that's what you...

STEPHEN. Okay, well... that's your... What the fuck is happening?!

FATHER PIERRE. Stephen, Dermot, Stephen – (*Laughs.*) When I was your age ...

STEPHEN (*interrupting*). No. No. You just... fuck off, you old bollocks.

LYDIA. Stephen...

STEPHEN. I'll take that... fucking stick and I'll...

DERMOT (*coming to* STEPHEN). Whoa, whoa, whoa...

FATHER PIERRE. You see this is... the dark one abides.

STEPHEN. You're the frigging dark one.

BRENDAN (*getting between* STEPHEN *and* DERMOT). Lads, lads, this is... maybe you should...

STEPHEN. Maybe should what?

BRENDAN. I don't know... Calm it down...

STEPHEN. I'll calm you fucking down! What are you doing in here anyway?

BRENDAN. What?

STEPHEN. Whatcha always sniffing around up here for?

BRENDAN. You told me to come up!

STEPHEN. No I didn't! When?

BRENDAN. 'Cause that cheque you gave me bounced!

STEPHEN. Yeah, but that's...

BRENDAN. You said to come up and get my money 'cause that cheque wasn't gonna...

STEPHEN. Yeah, well, that's...

BRENDAN. Fucking pay me and I'll go.

DERMOT. Yeah, alright, Brendan.

STEPHEN. Yeah, well, I'll... Anyway, you're just a fucking...

BRENDAN. A what?

LYDIA. Brendan...

STEPHEN. I'm on to you. I know what you're after – yeah – pick someone who knows how to look out for herself.

BILLIE. What do you mean by that?

STEPHEN. Someone who knows how to live for herself and...

BILLIE. I know how to live!

STEPHEN. Someone who's...

BILLIE. What...

DERMOT. He means someone normal.

BILLIE. I'm normal.

DERMOT. Billie, you're super-normal. You're beyond normal. He means someone who's normal-normal.

BILLIE. You mean someone who's not...

Advancing on DERMOT, *attacking him.*

Youse are all gone in your fucking heads. And none a youse is worth one animal. The chickens. They had a whole life – a whole world. An old dog has more love in his heart than all a youse put together.

As STEPHEN *and* BRENDAN *pull* BILLIE *away from* DERMOT.

They don't even know who you are – they just love your presence! They can feel your presence. And they know you have a soul. They know. But I never understand what you're saying.

DERMOT *falls backwards against a table and on to the floor.*

I understand a dog barking. But I don't understand any of youse. I never do!

FATHER PIERRE. What's happened, I'm...

ELIZABETH. It's alright.

BILLIE. Youse have all reached that age, not me, where death has come and touched you. You might not be old people, but you're all like someone who's been stabbed, you can run along for a little while, but death has touched you. I see it everywhere – the bags under people's eyes, the denial your hair is gone.

STEPHEN *is trying to help* DERMOT *up.* FATHER PIERRE *is smiling. Looking at his hands.*

DERMOT. I can't get up.

STEPHEN. He's alright. Here, what's wrong with you?

DERMOT (*laughs*). I'm, my... I can't...

STEPHEN. What, get up!

BILLIE. I didn't do anything to him.

STEPHEN *and* LYDIA *try to help* DERMOT *up, they pull him by the arms. He staggers to his feet but falls, having no strength in his legs.*

FATHER PIERRE. No, I...

DERMOT. I can't. I can't feel my... Where's my... Something's happened to my...

Again LYDIA *and* STEPHEN, *and now* BILLIE, *try to help* DERMOT *to his feet, but his legs are useless.*

FATHER PIERRE *approaches* DERMOT.

FATHER PIERRE. Dermot...

DERMOT. Yeah, I'm...

FATHER PIERRE. No, Dermot, Dermot...

DERMOT. What…

FATHER PIERRE. I can see you.

> DERMOT *sits on the floor looking up at* FATHER PIERRE. FATHER PIERRE *looks around at everyone.*

> I can see you. I see you all! Thank God! Thank God! I can see!

FREYA (*lifting her arms and crying out in celebration*). 'Woohooooo!'

> *Lights.*

ACT FOUR

The lights rise to find BRENDAN *sitting at the piano, playing. A bag and a coat belonging to* STEPHEN *sit nearby.* BILLIE *comes in. She stands in the doorway watching* BRENDAN *silently.*

BILLIE. I was sorry about your mom.

BRENDAN. Oh hi.

BILLIE. I was sorry to hear about your mother.

   BRENDAN *stops playing.*

BRENDAN. Oh. Thanks. Yeah.

   BILLIE *brings the tray to the piano, putting it down.*

BILLIE. You found her.

BRENDAN. Yeah.

BILLIE. In the toilet?

BRENDAN. Yeah.

BILLIE. That must have been weird.

BRENDAN. Yeah, I thought maybe she'd fallen down, or collapsed, but... Yeah.

BILLIE. I'm sorry I wasn't at the funeral.

BRENDAN. That's okay.

BILLIE. No one told me when it was on.

BRENDAN. Yeah, I know, don't...

BILLIE. You play nice.

BRENDAN. Ah, I can't play. There was a piano in our bar. I used to get lessons. But not since I was in fourth class.

BILLIE. You living up there on your own now?

BRENDAN. Hm? Yeah.

BILLIE. What's it like? Must be nice?

BRENDAN. It's quiet. The same old lads come in. They don't say very much.

BILLIE. I'd say that's how you like it.

BRENDAN. It's always been like that. Big changes here.

BILLIE. My uncle is living here now – the priest.

BRENDAN. Mm.

BILLIE. People are gonna come here to live here and pray with him. People are coming today. They're gonna stay here and have a special mass. It's mad.

BRENDAN. Stephen's moving out.

BILLIE. Yeah. He's going.

BRENDAN. Yeah, he told me to wait here, he went to the bank to get me my money.

BILLIE. You're finally gonna get it.

BRENDAN. Yeah, I told him not to bother, but…

BILLIE. Yeah.

BRENDAN. You're not going with him? When he moves out?

BILLIE. Nah.

BRENDAN. You're happy enough here.

BILLIE. Here, listen, why don't I come up to you some evening? I could help you.

BRENDAN. Yeah?

BILLIE. You know I like you, Brendan.

BRENDAN. Yeah?

BILLIE. Yeah. I always do. You know that. I could help you. It wouldn't be quiet.

BRENDAN. That's for sure.

BILLIE. I'll come over. I can come tonight. I can come any night.

BRENDAN. Yeah... look, listen, you know Freya...

BILLIE. Who?

BRENDAN. Freya. Freya.

BILLIE. What about her?

BRENDAN. Yeah, she's she... You know. She comes and... So... she's... already helping me.

BILLIE. My uncle Dermot's Freya?

BRENDAN. Yeah.

BILLIE. That's young enough to be his daughter?

BRENDAN. Yeah, well, she's not... They're not... any more, they don't...

BILLIE. And she's coming up there with you?

BRENDAN. She has experience, you know, working behind a bar and she's...

BILLIE. Is she your girlfriend?

BRENDAN. I don't know.

BILLIE. You don't know? How do you not know something like that, Brendan.

BRENDAN. I don't know.

BILLIE. You don't know how you don't know? I mean, how fucking stupid are you, Brendan? 'I don't know how I don't know...' Like how fucking thick does that sound?

BRENDAN. Yeah.

BILLIE. How long has she been coming up there?

BRENDAN. She gave me a hand when my mum died.

BILLIE. She got in on the scene.

BRENDAN. She was... She helped me.

BILLIE. Oh. 'She helped me.' You saw how she was helping my uncle Dermot. Have you seen him now? He can't walk!

BRENDAN. Yeah, look, Billie, I…

BILLIE. I woulda helped you, Brendan, all you had to do was say, 'Help me,' I help everybody.

BRENDAN. I know.

BILLIE. You do know about her, about Freya, don't ya? Even her own mother knew it. Tried to tell people. Said she'd been changed out. And look what happened to her. Her mother is in the mental hospital in Ballinasloe. That's what they do.

BRENDAN. What who does?

BILLIE. What they do. She's one of them.

BRENDAN. One of who?

BILLIE. Don't make me say it. You're gonna make me look like I'm mad as well. You know what I mean. I dreamed about her – I saw her – she was in there, under the hawthorn and the rocks and the little brown streams you can only hear in the ditch, even in under the all old graves, she's been all in under there, you can't smell it? You don't smell that off her?

BRENDAN. Her house is damp.

BILLIE. Her house is damp, my fuck. You can't even see she's had a million faces and she's gonna do you next now that your mother's gone and there's no more rosaries being said up there. But you 'don't know', though, do you? You don't know what madness is or where you go when it gets you. It's a whole other world. You don't know though. How alone you are now, and how tired you're gonna be.

BRENDAN. Billie.

BILLIE. I'm not interested, Brendan. You can keep all that shit outta here. It's a good thing there's gonna be mass here all the time. That's all I can say.

BRENDAN. Billie. I'm sorry. You know I like you.

BILLIE. Who cares? Nobody cares, Brendan.

BRENDAN. I do want us to be friends.

BILLIE. Well, I'm not able to do that.

She turns away from him. He stands looking at her helplessly. He reaches to take his anorak from the piano as LYDIA *comes in, helping* DERMOT, *who walks with two sticks.*

LYDIA. Oh hello. Stephen about?

BRENDAN. He's on his way from the bank.

DERMOT. There you are, Brendan. Good man.

BRENDAN. Do you need a hand?

DERMOT. No! I'm grand, I'll be grand, Billie, here you wouldn't...

LYDIA *brings a chair to* DERMOT. *He gratefully perches on the edge of it.*

I was sorry to hear about your ma, Brendan.

BRENDAN. Thanks.

DERMOT. Very sudden.

BRENDAN. Yeah.

DERMOT. I woulda been at the funeral, only...

BRENDAN. Yeah, I know, thanks.

LYDIA. It was lovely.

BRENDAN. Yeah, it was very nice. She woulda been very pleased, I think.

LYDIA. Oh yes. And the music. Did you pick all of that?

BRENDAN. Yeah.

BILLIE. Freya helped him.

BRENDAN (*quickly*). How is your, do they know what...

DERMOT. It's a lack of weakness. A lack of...

LYDIA. A lack of power.

DERMOT. A lack of power in the...

LYDIA. Lumbar...

DERMOT. Pelvic...

DERMOT. Just need to rest it up. No problem.

BRENDAN. Oh right.

DERMOT. It's unusual. But I'm unusual. And I'll tell you – this way of getting about – with the sticks? Man, it builds up your arms. Look at me! Look at that. Like a man half my age now.

BRENDAN. Yeah.

DERMOT. Billie, is there anything to drink?

BILLIE. Father Pierre won't allow it.

DERMOT. What?

BILLIE. This is a house of retreat now.

DERMOT. Oh yeah, Jaysus.

BILLIE. What like, you didn't know that?

DERMOT. I just didn't know there was no drink involved.

BILLIE. Yeah, nobody knows anything.

DERMOT. For fuck's sake, Billie, don't keep wangalising on about everything all the frigging time, will you?

LYDIA. The place is falling down, Billie.

BILLIE. So sell it! Move us into a flat! Turning the place into some kind of looney convent for a load of Jesus lose-bags…

DERMOT. There's money in religion, Billie. I'm telling you, the old fucker is on to something.

BILLIE. I don't think you even care about religion. You're just doing this to me and Stephen so you can stink us out and not give us anything.

DERMOT. Why would I even do that?

BILLIE. Why do you do anything? 'Cause you hate people. You always did. That's why you're the way you are now – you're being punished.

DERMOT. I've just lost some power in my back – or else my legs – I just need to rest!

ACT FOUR   93

BILLIE. Nah, you're a picture of your soul. And you as well, Lydia.

LYDIA. What did I do?

BILLIE. You tell me. You're stuck with him, like a sad old fucking nursemaid.

LYDIA. He's my husband.

BILLIE. Exactly. You're a fucking eejit.

ELIZABETH *comes through with* FATHER PIERRE.

FATHER PIERRE (*clear-sighted, pointedly addressing each person*). Hello, hello, hello. Hello, Billie, and hello, Dermot, and hello, Lydia, and hello...

BRENDAN. Brendan.

FATHER PIERRE. That's right. Look at you all. My apologies if you've been waiting for me. I needed to replenish my wardrobe. I haven't seen myself in many years, and had no idea how Elizabeth was dressing me! Ha ha! No, I'm only joking of course, she did her best – she always does. But by God, now that our first pilgrims will be arriving and I thank you that you've all joined me to celebrate, and their deposits are safely on... deposit, I can assure you this house will be reborn now.

STEPHEN *comes in wearing a suit.*

Ah, Stephen, my friend. I was just saying how this house is about to be reborn.

ELIZABETH. Stay. Stay to see it.

STEPHEN. I can't. I'm sorry.

DERMOT. Father, tell us, what did they say about your eyes?

FATHER PIERRE. Where?

DERMOT. In your head.

ELIZABETH. In Sligo general hospital.

FATHER PIERRE. Oh yes. The top man there, he isn't usually there, he's more a psychologist than an ophthalmologist, he was only home from Dublin on his holidays by chance, but they got him in to look at me and what he was saying was it turns out that it was a kind of force of psychology – like I was willing myself not to see. 'Cause I couldn't bear what I was seeing! I could actually *see* all along – but I just couldn't accept what I was seeing so I didn't see it. Isn't that fascinating?

STEPHEN. Not really.

ELIZABETH. Stephen.

STEPHEN. No, I just mean, I totally understand that. It makes sense.

FATHER PIERRE. What a waste of all that time! Can you imagine? Poor Elizabeth.

Following ELIZABETH *out to the kitchen.*

Ah well. Yes – he's going to get a brilliant student from Trinity to come and interview me for a paper they want to give at some conference in Lucerne next summer.

DERMOT. Stephen does that.

STEPHEN. Does what?

DERMOT. Won't see things.

STEPHEN. Yeah, must run in the family.

FATHER PIERRE (*off*). You know, I actually believe that it was coming here, coming home, that lifted the veil from my eyes. It was the final piece of the puzzle. You know I saw the Virgin Mary one time out there – on the hedge! Up on the hedge. I knelt down in the ditch.

DERMOT (*calling to* FATHER PIERRE). It's the same with me. I think what's happened my legs is that I'm being forced to rest, you see. Forced to take a break from running around after everyb–

He stops talking as FREYA *comes in.*

FREYA. Hello.

DERMOT. Freya.

She looks to BRENDAN.

FREYA. Are you ready?

BRENDAN. What? Yeah, I… eh…

He looks at STEPHEN.

STEPHEN. Oh yeah, here…

STEPHEN *gestures him to come.* BRENDAN *follows* STEPHEN *out.*

FREYA *stands awkwardly. She seems to have lost all confidence.*

FREYA. How are you, Mrs McFaddin?

LYDIA. Yes. I'm fine.

FREYA. Mr McFaddin.

DERMOT. I'm terrific. How are you?

FREYA. Yeah, I'm…

DERMOT. How is your ma?

FREYA. Much better thanks. She's home.

DERMOT. Oh. Well, isn't that…

FREYA. Yeah. It's good to have her now.

DERMOT. Great. She's home. And out of Ballinasloe.

FREYA. Yeah. I'm minding her now.

DERMOT. That's… You're… Yep.

FREYA. I'm sorry I missed a lot of work. I'm available if you… I'm very happy to come in any day, Saturdays or Sundays are fine as well.

DERMOT. Okay, well. That's…

FREYA. We had a lot of… since my sister was gone and… my ma was confused and things were… but she's a lot better now so… and I want to apologise to you, Mrs McFaddin.

LYDIA. Okay.

FREYA. I'm aware there's been a lot of turmoil because of… and… I don't remember a huge amount but I know there was… and I was… well, I've taken the pledge. And I'm…

LYDIA. Alright.

DERMOT. You've taken the pledge.

FREYA. A pledge of abstinence.

DERMOT. No. You're a good girl.

FREYA. I'm very sorry.

DERMOT. No, no. Sure, look. But you're good, that's the…

FREYA. I'm, yeah, no, I'm…

ELIZABETH *carries in drinks on a tray as* STEPHEN *and* BRENDAN *return.*

ELIZABETH. Oh, stay, Stephen. Pierre needs you here. We all need you.

DERMOT. Where are you fucking going anyway?

STEPHEN. Glasgow.

DERMOT. Fucking Glasgow?! You'll be back here in about a week, just watch!

ELIZABETH. Yes, just stay here.

She links STEPHEN*'s arm.*

We could use the help – and I could use it.

STEPHEN (*suddenly pulling away roughly*). Just fucking let me go, will you? Sorry. I'm sorry.

FATHER PIERRE. Stephen. Are you alright?

STEPHEN. Yeah, no I'm…

BRENDAN. I… (*Indicating he will leave.*)

FATHER PIERRE. Please, no, Bernard. Help us toast the arrival of our first pilgrims, give him a glass and for Frieda. Do we all have a drink? Lovely.

He suddenly winces at a pain in his shoulders.

LYDIA. Are you alright?

FATHER PIERRE. I'm fantastic. (*To* LYDIA.) You see this cravat? It's silk. Oh my G... what a journey. To think where I was only a few months ago and now we stand virtually on the establishment of a – I won't say a new church, but certainly something close to the one true Church.

Now that I can see again, I, em... I apprehend everything in a new... I mean what if this life, rather than just torture, as I had imagined it, all this suffering of pain and death – and ceasing to be – what if it's all, in fact, the most beautiful *sacrifice*, mm? That each of us has the privilege to offer?

To turn to God, broken, and offer Him our *broken*, *humbled*, *humiliated* spirit – shorn of dignity – isn't that, in fact, the purest gift of thanks one could give, in return for...

BILLIE. In return for what?

FATHER PIERRE. In return for everything.

DERMOT*'s leg is shaking.*

LYDIA. What's wrong with you?

DERMOT (*looking down at his legs*). I'm after going to the toilet.

LYDIA *goes to him.*

(*Shrugging her away.*) I'm alright!

DERMOT *struggles to make his way out on his sticks. He can't make it, slowly sinking to the floor.*

FATHER PIERRE. Help him someone. Billie.

BILLIE. I'm not getting wee on me.

BRENDAN (*going to help* DERMOT). Here. You're alright.

FREYA *is going out.*

DERMOT. Freya.

But she's gone.

ELIZABETH. You won't get wee on you, Billie. Help me.

ELIZABETH, BILLIE *and* BRENDAN *carry* DERMOT *out*.

DERMOT. Youse don't have to carry me, for fuck's sake! I can walk!

ELIZABETH. Someone get the doors!

FATHER PIERRE. Oh yes.

FATHER PIERRE *goes*.

LYDIA. You think we did it to him?

STEPHEN. What.

LYDIA. The water from the little tap. Maybe no one needs it twice.

STEPHEN. Fuck knows.

LYDIA. You're just gonna walk away from us all?

STEPHEN. What else can I do? I can't stay here.

LYDIA. And I can't help loving him. I can't stop it.

STEPHEN. Who chooses who they love anyway?

LYDIA *comes to him*.

LYDIA. Well, maybe if you hadna given me the water I'd a been free to wander into a different trap. Or at least one I understood.

STEPHEN (*a shrug*). Hm.

LYDIA. You know what's mad? Under all the... under the magic or the spell or the illusion or whatever it is. I can feel you under here. Under it all. You are in here somewhere.

STEPHEN. Under all the brambles.

LYDIA. It's true. Maybe if you could stay somehow...

STEPHEN. I can't. Where?

LYDIA. Out there, take up Pierre's offer – let them do it up like a nice apartment you could still live here.

STEPHEN. For what?

LYDIA. I don't know. For something. Something. I...

DERMOT. Lydia.

She turns to see DERMOT *standing there on his sticks.*

Tell them to leave me alone, would ya?

LYDIA. Can you stand?

DERMOT. Look at me. I'm standing.

LYDIA. You don't look so good. I'll get the chair.

She goes.

DERMOT. Don't get the chair. I don't need the chair. (*To* STEPHEN.) I suppose you can't fight destiny. And turns out I fucking need her. Condemned to need her now. Will you be alright?

STEPHEN *nods.*

I'm gonna get better, this is just...

LYDIA *comes in with a wheelchair.*

I don't need the chair! I told you! I can walk!

He tries, but he can't.

LYDIA. Get in the chair! Just get in the chair!

DERMOT. Alright! Jaysus! I'm in it. I'm in it. (*Pitifully.*) I want to go home.

LYDIA *nods.*

LYDIA (*to* STEPHEN). I'll see you.

LYDIA *brings* DERMOT *out.* STEPHEN *picks up a bag and his coat.*

BILLIE *comes in.*

BILLIE. Pierre is gonna say a prayer in the garden. Down at the gate. The new people will be here soon.

STEPHEN *nods.*

Can we talk about trains?

STEPHEN *shakes his head*.

You're gonna get the train, aren't you?

STEPHEN *nods*.

You lucky fucker. You won't take me with you?

STEPHEN. I'm no good for you, Billie.

BILLIE. I don't know how you can say that.

STEPHEN. I can't look after you.

BILLIE. But you do. You always do.

STEPHEN. But I can't any more. I just can't do it. I can't talk about trains all the time. I can't wait when you go into town wondering what's happened to you. I can't just give you every day helping you find everything you keep losing 'cause I'm living on the edge of your next frigging meltdown.

BILLIE. I won't. I won't melt down.

STEPHEN. But you do. You just do.

BILLIE. But I won't. I'm telling you, I won't. If you take me with you, I'll never do it again. I won't hit you. I won't shout.

STEPHEN. But I don't think you're able not to.

BILLIE. It's not like against you – I don't mean it 'cause I don't like you – it's just what happens.

STEPHEN. Yeah, but you don't hit people in the street or people in shops or someone you want something off.

BILLIE. That's because I feel safe with you.

STEPHEN. But do you not see what it costs me? Can you not see what you're doing to me?

BILLIE. I don't mean it.

STEPHEN. It doesn't matter! I feel like I'm getting old. I feel like I'm dying!

BILLIE. I'm not doing that to you.

STEPHEN. Just leave me alone, will ya?

BILLIE. What?

ACT FOUR   101

STEPHEN. Just leave me alone!

BILLIE. Stephen...

STEPHEN. What? What!!

BILLIE. No nothing, I...

STEPHEN. What?!

BILLIE. Nothing.

STEPHEN. I'll write to you and I'll let you know how I'm getting on. These'll mind you better than me, anyway. Elizabeth is organised. And there'll be people coming through here and you can get on with your life. And mind the place. Honestly. It'll all be better anyway.

BILLIE. You'll never come back. I know you won't.

STEPHEN. Well, we'll just... Just give it a chance.

BILLIE (*shakes her head*). You'll bury the memory of love. 'Cause that's what it is, you know. The memory of how I climbed into your lap and we'd sit in the light of the window and laugh about nothing.

You won't even remember my face in the end. Life will be too difficult if you remember so you won't remember. And even when you're old and you haven't seen me for thirty years and you come home to Ireland to collect my things and they tell you how it was for me at the end, how my trips to the hospital became more frequent and prolonged, you'll suddenly have a vague recollection of my face, but you won't allow yourself to really see me there.

No, instead, you'll take my things in a plastic bag and sit on a cold steel bench beside a bin in the railway station and you'll look up at the timetable and you'll marvel at how alien the world feels – the human world of travel and clocks and the endless illusions of arriving, and you'll remark to yourself how meaningless it all is.

But you'll know, somewhere in the darkness there's a quieter, hidden fear: that perhaps it *does* all mean something. That perhaps it's all this simple: you really knew me.

And I really knew you. And in those moments, in each other, we saw the face of God. And once seen it's never really banished. From your heart. Not really. And you'll wonder about your own end.

Will you be alone? Will it perhaps be by your own hand? It's not inconceivable. And for a brief moment you'll suspect that everything will be alright, because you'll suspect that even then, right at the end, I will be there. And I will hold your hand. And I will forgive you.

But you'll also banish these thoughts. You'll have to. And you'll remember how much of living is really just forgetting.

She comes to him and stands there, holding his hand. STEPHEN *finally raises his eyes and looks at her, full in the face. She embraces him.*

After a moment, STEPHEN *goes, and* LYDIA *comes in carrying some food and plates on a tray.*

LYDIA. Put these up the far end.

BILLIE. Can we talk?

LYDIA. Set the table and you can talk about whatever you want.

BILLIE. You start.

LYDIA. Okay. Stations.

BILLIE. Mm-hm.

LYDIA. Limerick Junction.

BILLIE. Yeah.

LYDIA. Talk to me.

BILLIE. There's no town there. Just a station. No one lives there. No one stays there, you just transfer.

LYDIA. You come and go.

BILLIE. Yeah, go anywhere. Like to a real place.

LYDIA. Escape anywhere.

BILLIE. Yeah, no one would know which way you went.

LYDIA (*frowns*). There's no town there?

BILLIE. There's nothing there. It's the middle of Tipperary. It's like a magic door. Get yourself a ticket to Limerick Junction, change platforms, and poof – you're gone!

LYDIA. Boom.

BILLIE. Shoot across to Rosslare Harbour. Ferry to Le Havre. SNCF to Paris, Orient Express to Istanbul – if you don't mind changing at Bucharest.

LYDIA. I don't mind.

BILLIE. Okay – well, once a week I think it is – there's a service to Tehran. Get yourself down there – through Iran, across Pakistan, bang, down into New Delhi, on to Varanasi. You know what's there, of course?

LYDIA. No.

BILLIE. In Varanasi? The Manikarnika Ghat. Where the steps lead down to the River Ganges. They cremate the bodies of the dead there twenty-four hours a day, seven days a week. You wanna be cremated there, Lydia, you know why?

LYDIA. Why?

BILLIE. 'Cause if you're burned there and your bones are thrown in the River Ganges – you won't be reincarnated any more, you're free. Your soul is washed clean, and you finally return to nothingness. With none of this life stuck on you any more.

LYDIA. I must do that then.

BILLIE. Yeah.

Lights.

www.nickhernbooks.co.uk

@nickhernbooks